M.A.G.I.C.™ at Work
5 Forces for Powerful Organizations

Nancy Noble, PhD

M.A.G.I.C.™ at Work
5 Forces for Powerful Organizations
url: www.noblealignments.com

Library of Congress Cataloging-in-Publication Data:

Noble, Nancy K., 1957 –
M.A.G.I.C.™ at Work: 5 Forces for Powerful Organizations/ by
Nancy Noble, PhD
Includes bibliographical references.

ISBN: 978-1-77277-018-6

1. Management. 2. Consulting. 3. Organizational
Effectiveness. 4. Human Resources.

Contents

Gratitude   vii

About this Book   xi

Chapter 1: My Journey Into Organizational Alchemy   1

Chapter 2: The Foundations of Organizational Alchemy   13

Chapter 3: Master Conversations for Peak Performance   21

Chapter 4: Align Goals, Roles and Teams   43

Chapter 5: Grow Talent and Leadership   59

Chapter 6: Ignite Active Engagement   89

Chapter 7: Change Readily - Well T.I.M.E.D.!   101

Chapter 8: The Person and Mindset of the

Organizational Alchemist   113

Is Your Organization M.A.G.I.C.?   121

Bibliography   125

Gratitude

Hold it! Don't turn the page just because you discover this is the traditional "Acknowledgements" section.

There is a chapter in this book I'll give you permission to skip if you want......**But not this one.** No one ever became a master at any craft without a lot of other people to discipline, encourage and teach them. I can't call myself a master just yet, but there are a host of such masters who have been there for me. And in life, if there is one thing I have learned, it is to be always grateful. Whatever you may decide about this book, the following people deserve your attention and respect. There are no well-known celebrities in the list – yet – but they are my heroes. They did everything in their power to teach me, so if you don't like this book, it is definitely NOT their fault! You'll see a few of them referred to again later in the book, but here goes…

Danna Wessels, my sweet partner and spouse of more than two decades. We have had great fun and we have successfully battled together even the prospect of early death. She has been completely supportive in my career dramas as much as the successes. Look for her book, *Danna's Dust*, about her war with cancer.

Jeanne-Marie Bowman, my unwavering friend and ever supportive, patient AND tough mentor. It has been said (a bit unclear by whom), "When the student is ready, the teacher will appear." She was that teacher. After many years of working together, we left Austin, Texas the very same week to go after our next stage of mastery. Today, from across the globe, we look again to partner in helping leaders and organizations achieve all they envision.

Now it becomes hard to know where to start, so I'll go chronologically from earliest times to latest. Way back in my teen and college years, the Guthrie, Satterfield, Tanner, Miller, Price, Craig and Storm families served as my adoptive parents and siblings when my own family was enduring some tough stuff. We did mission trips in Mexico and hiking trips in the mountains together. None of us had any idea that those were the seeds of much larger efforts I got to be involved with later. Thank you.

Dr. Gary Noble, whose name I just had to keep, even after divorce. The name worked nicely with my first name, and the memory of growing up with such a sweet man, through college and eleven years of marriage just could not be tossed. Thank you.

Ed and Linda Smith, and a great host of people at the Richardson Heights Baptist Church in Texas, where I further practiced event and educational programming, opened a counseling office and 'cut my teeth' on organizational politics and stakeholder management. Thank you.

Unspeakable gratitude to Jay W. Thomas and Thomas J. Thomas, of Opposite Strengths. Their funding of my dissertation research ensured that I got that Ph.D. added to my name. Before that, their model helped me do some maturing and understanding of myself and others Thank you.

Dixie Tischler, Ralph Gohring and Austan Librach, among many others, who gave me those opportunities at the City of Austin. In municipal government, where many might perceive limited ability to be creative, they let me experiment and take risks, and to forgive when a few of those experiments may have caused them embarrassment. For the most part, we had some great days together. It was also during those days that I met Carol Kerr Welch, who later introduced me to Jeanne-Marie. Thank You.

From Motorola and Freescale days there are so many to thank I am very certain to leave someone out, so please forgive me if your name isn't here. Gary Langley, who gave me the huge opportunity to move into the corporate sector when others had doubted my capability there. Amy Owen and Russ Robinson– the most notable of my peers. Brett Rodgers, Laurie Hahn, Jennifer Swenson, Maria Grahl, Henry Olejnik, Todd Nalodka, Drew Morton, Andy Handy, Maria Garrett, Finnoula Barrie and many other HR colleagues and friends. Brett helped me win over some tough clients in the manufacturing space and was a shoulder to lean on several times. Laurie seemed always to say the right thing when I was at a moment of emotional, political, or even physical challenge. Drew was a patient and supportive manager during one of the hardest periods of my years in that company, and he, too, let me do some experimenting that worked out magically. Jennifer Swenson, we got to see the world together, albeit in a hurry, and still some of my favorite memories. Arlynn Budd, the most fun administrative assistant ever, and a lasting friend. Thank You.

Chekib Akrout, Chris Belden, and Dave Mothersole were among my favorite clients in those Motorola and Freescale days. With them, I learned some of the needs of very senior executives, traveled the world, facilitated significant changes and stretched my capabilities. Thank you.

David Doolittle, Motorola and Freescale Human Resources VP who left us too early, was both inspiring and challenging. He taught me that "process will never replace leadership," and that

Nancy Noble, PhD

"the best way to develop someone is just before they are ready." Thank you.

At Covidien and Medtronic, I worked with clients like Kris Wagner, Pete Wehrly, Bryan Hanson, Stacy Enxing Seng, Jacqueline Strayer, Jim Willett and Wayde McMillan. These people again gave me multiple opportunities and challenged me. Beside me in those efforts were great partners from HR. Melody Sian, Tracy Sinclair, Jamie Valpatic, Melissa Uribes, Marc Assante, Alejandra Bailon, Kerry Tehan and Merryl Rees were my friends, co-consultants, and often 'co-conspirators' in the effort to help leaders build powerful organizations. Thank you.

Sandra McNeill, without whom I might not have been so fortunate as to move to Colorado. None of us knew, then, how much we would need to be here, both for the generous employer that Covidien was and for the quality of care the Bone Marrow Transplant team at CU Hospital would provide during Danna's greatest challenge. Nor would I have met Joe Gibbons, Kate Hoepfner-Karle, Mike Dunford, Janice Deskus, or Ralph Mills, all HR leaders who opened big doors for me, had my back and provided excellent partnership in a variety of projects. They also put in good words for me during the process of selecting people to help with the integration of Medtronic and Covidien, which then resulted in an offer to either stay in a great Organization Development role or to take a great severance that would allow me to go independent and write this book. Finally, Matt Walter, Patty McPhee, Tracy Platt and Jodi Guthrie, who helped make the integration into Medtronic smoother, and leaving it much harder than I had first thought.

THANK YOU. THANK YOU. THANK YOU.

May your lives and work always look and feel like magic!

x

About This Book

I have written this book as an introduction to the critical forces driving organizational success. It is not really a field guide or operating manual, although I do offer a few tools and step-by-step process instructions. The intent is to give business owners, corporate leaders, managers, Human Resources professionals, consultants and others some beginning concepts to help them build more effective and profitable organizations.

You can read it cover-to-cover, which I have personally rarely done with books like this. Or, you can take the little assessment in the back of the book and select key chapters for focus based on your scores. Finally, you can simply pick the chapters that strike you as most helpful to you and your company at this point in its story. It's your choice. While working M.A.G.I.C.™ requires discipline and practice, and the first two components are the most foundational, it is not a linear process. It is a framework and a mindset.

Here is a brief description of each chapter to guide you:

Chapter 1: My Journey into Organizational Alchemy and M.A.G.I.C.™
I go through most of my personal and professional history here, unfolding the progression of how I learned this craft at every phase in my own life. It is intended to ask you to think about your own history and the formation of your own skillset and personal "magic".

Chapter 2: The Foundations of Organizational Alchemy
If you just can't get into mystical, metaphorical, "woo-woo" thinking, just skip this chapter. It is a brief review of alchemy, the precursor of modern chemistry, and how its elements and theories relate to business and organizational effectiveness. *In a nutshell, both focus on transformation.* I wrote it to provoke some thinking that is a bit different than the more typical business book, and to rationalize my choice of the M.A.G.I.C.™ acronym to characterize my framework

Chapter 3: Master Conversations for Top Performance
The point of this chapter is that people in organizations have to talk to each other. No amount of process, policy, tools or structure will replace human dialogue. Covered here are the necessary components of effective workplace conversations, and several types of conversations common in the business context, including tough/corrective conversations, development conversations, career conversations, performance conversations, the 1-on-1 meeting and team conversations.

Chapter 4: Align Goals, Roles and Teams
THE fundamental operating principle for a powerful organization is that of *alignment.* This chapter offers description and direction for aligning vision, strategy and annual goals, for designing organizational structures that keep roles clear and aligned, and for aligning teams so they can be productive without distraction and confusion from internal mis-alignments.

Chapter 5: Grow Talent and Leadership
Talent Management practices are the primary focus of this chapter. Based in the broader business strategy, the practices outlined include critical position profiling, talent review processes/meetings, new leader integration, and a discussion of the roles of coach, mentor and sponsor. Personality and leadership assessments are the final discussion, emphasizing

why and when to use them, and describing a few more common (and some not so common) approaches.

Chapter 6: Ignite Active Engagement
I go a little crazy with the acronyms in this chapter, in order to outline key principles for ensuring high engagement among employees. F.I.R.E. defines the characteristics of highly engaged employees. F.U.E.L. outlines what really ignites engagement. Finally, there is a description of those conditions that can S.M.O.T.H.E.R. engagement.

Chapter 7: Change Readily – well T.I.M.E.D.!
In this chapter, we close out the formula with descriptions of the timing and rationale for key organizational changes, critical leadership behaviors required during change, and the tactical framework and components of effective change management plans. Discussed also is stakeholder management, the core of successful change efforts.

Chapter 8: The Person and Mindset of the Organizational Alchemist
While the M.A.G.I.C. formula is composed of many practices and processes for doing the work of Organizational Alchemy, the person and mindset of the Alchemist is what makes all those practices and processes successful. In this chapter, described are the required qualities and competencies of confidentiality, "hero by proxy," fearlessness, positive expectation, curious observation, synthesis, awareness of larger impact, and political/organizational savvy.

Assessment: Is Your Organization M.A.G.I.C.?
Use this 25-item questionnaire to assess which of the five M.A.G.I.C. forces your organization is doing well, and where you need to give more attention.

Chapter 1
My Journey into Organizational Alchemy

I'm no Harry Potter – I don't know anything about 'slight of hand' or illusion, like the guys on stage in Vegas. I certainly know nothing about wizardry. I have not read every single Harry Potter book, though I have seen all the movies. I never had a magic kit as a kid. But, I do love the concept behind all this stuff about sorcery, alchemy, magic – the idea that we can create something really great by only using very basic, even defective materials, *and our minds*. I love the miracle stories in the Bible, like Moses taking his people through the Dead Sea on dry land, Jesus turning water into wine, or feeding thousands of people with only a few loaves of bread and a couple of fish. "The Sword in the Stone" was one of my favorite childhood movies. Stories of alchemists, who could turn rocks into fine gold, and their secret schools and apprenticeships make my head spin with imagination, fascination and awe! I really never thought I could do any of this, although I have grown over life to believe that my thoughts can change anything, and I have seen thousands of less spectacular miracles in life, as well as a couple perhaps equally spectacular.

So, imagine my surprise and delight when, as I worked in very bureaucratic environments throughout life, where "magic" is not viewed as rational, measurable, repeatable, people began to call on me and depend on me to work a sort of magic of my own. They actually would see me as a kind of wizard, and even say that to me! They would ask me to come and "do my magic" with their organizational structures, their teams, their strategies, their changes, etc.

What they were really acknowledging was that, perhaps like the alchemists, I had no magic. Rather, I had a skillset -- a PRACTICED skillset, and a MINDSET. So now, I get to have the fun of sharing that skillset and mindset with you…. So you, too, can become an alchemist in your own little world – the M.A.G.I.C.™ of Organizational Alchemy!

Harry Potter, move over. Corporate America has its own demons and monsters to slay, and they affect far more people. I expect this book won't likely sell nearly so well as J.K. Rowlings', but in the right hands, it could have enormous impact, and work true magic – at work!

Before we dive into that, it might help to share with you the back-story. It is a little self-serving, but I do want you to understand my growth into "organizational alchemy," as I believe it will prompt you to think of your own. I've organized the story according to the process many craftsmen follow in their journey to mastery….

The Novice Years

I had some family challenges as a child, including my mother's mental illness and the death of my father when I was 12 years old. So, my family life was a bit chaotic. Thankfully, I found that participation in youth activities at my church provided much of the structure, recognition and social involvement that helped me grow and mature. Over time, I became involved as a leader of some activities and learned how teams and organizations can accomplish far bigger things than any of the single individuals involved could do.

Perhaps the activities with the most impact were the summer mission trips I participated in as a high school student. These projects included about 100 teenagers and their 20-odd adult sponsors. We would distribute ourselves among 3-5 small communities just south of the Mexico border, conducting morning Bible study and crafts classes with the women, then afternoon Bible schools with the children, closing out the evenings with big open community church services. We would do this for 1-2 weeks each summer.

You can imagine what kind of leadership, coordination, project management, meeting management, materials management, program design, organizational structure and team work that required, not to mention sales and marketing! And I was the youth lead for 2 of those summer trips! Wow! Those were such awesome experiences. Not only did I learn how to do all these things, but I learned the value of being involved in something bigger than myself. Yes, I experienced all the drama and conflict, the fun, the spiritual glow, and the personal satisfaction of helping others. But the biggest thing I learned was that organized groups of people achieve huge things when they have all (or even just most) of the right pieces in place! And I experienced first hand the kind of energizing engagement you can feel, and act on, when you have excellent mentors and you love to be around the people you are working with. I did not know it at the time, of course, but those days were a model foreshadowing of the kind of impact I would have in more "sophisticated" environments as I grew as a person and as a consultant/practitioner.

Apprenticeship and Discovery

I had a great time as a college student, attending Baylor University, gaining a business degree. Yes, I continued religious activity there, both on campus and in the local church I had joined in town. During my first semester, I met Gary, the young pre-dental student I would marry right after graduation. We were both very religious and very active in religious activity. He actually became the president of the Baptist Student Union our senior year.

After graduation and marriage, while Gary went to dental school, I floundered with a couple of attempts to join the corporate world. I spent about 6 months opening new accounts for people at a local bank. The next six months, I worked for an insurance actuary in downtown Dallas. I just could not get excited about these positions. What I knew about was church and religious activity, and I really wanted to be doing that. In that time, the church we had joined brought in a new recreation minister who would oversee building a facility and establishing all kinds of recreational activities. Having worked in the church recreation center during high school, it became my goal to work in this new facility, and so I did! This facility was first rate for its time. There were two handball/racquetball courts, a weight room, showers, a running track on the second floor (which also served as the hallway between educational classrooms), and a full-size gymnasium, which also doubled as a roller skating rink. The building also housed the church's fellowship hall and kitchen. I worked as the receptionist for the building, and administrative assistant to the minister. Gary actually got a part-time job there, too, as recreational assistant. We made sure everyone upheld the rules and kept the peace, a very important task in such a new facility and environment. We took care of all the equipment, kept the place organized, supervised special events, even filled the soda machines and re-finished the gym/skating floor every 4-6 months. But the most fun thing I remember about that job was a kids' summer day camp I created and led, called the B.E.A.R. Club. (Bible, Education, Activities and Recreation). This was a multi-week camp for pre-teens. I recruited a few older teens to assist, and we had roughly 25 kids participate. I organized the whole thing. The educational time, the outings, the crafts, the budget, everything. The program was a wild hit – another confirmation and prediction that organizations were in my future, although the religious environment was not.

Gary and I continued working at the recreation center through his dental school years. We also became very close to the youth minister and his wife, and worked heavily with teenagers. I particularly loved working with them, so my next job was working for the youth minister. My primary responsibilities were again administrative, but I also had a variety of responsibilities related to 7th – 12th graders. These were great years where I was able to express lots of my creativity and love for orchestrating events and activities. I remember a few things, like annual girls' retreats that grew to over 100 girls over the 4 years I conducted them. I had either a leadership role or full responsibility for several mission trips, some more locally, others in Mexico.

While all this was happening, Gary's practice was growing, and I became restless in the positions I had. I wanted more responsibility, a title, better salary, etc. So, I left my full time position and entered the Baptist seminary in Fort Worth, first considering youth work as my primary 'calling.' I continued volunteering with the youth groups, and commuted daily to Fort Worth for classes. Within the first year, a new program was announced, in marriage and family counseling. This very much intrigued me. I had great interest in psychology, but had shied away from it during the college years, going for the more practical business degree. This degree appeared it would give me some options, and as in most cases of those who study psychology, I had some of my own internal struggles I was trying to understand (though they were below consciousness for a few more years). I was hoping the counseling degree would allow me to become a counselor in my own practice, teach or work in a church, or all of those. It seemed to offer flexibility for me as a woman considering ministry in a Christian denomination unfriendly to women in ministerial leadership roles. This would ultimately become the least of my concerns.

These were great years as well. I loved studying psychology, and was able to expand my programming creativity at the church, by creating a 6-week program for couples based on one of the books I was studying. I also got to host this great evening program for couples, another of my first "large group" facilitated events! This program involved setting up the fellowship hall for a really nice romantic dinner, with violinist, candles, tables for two, a lovely 4-course meal, the whole environment for great intimate conversation. Then Gary and I would trade off prompting the couples' dialogues with questions like, "Talk about the most fun date you had before marriage." Or, "Tell each other the 3 things you most love about the other, and why. Take 5 minutes per person to do this." These were very successful and fun events the couples very much appreciated. Many had young children, so we had even worked out childcare in the nursery, quite a luxury for young parents.

A Masters' degree became a PhD in Counseling Psychology. I set up a counseling center at our church. I became a grader for my major professor and head of the psychology department. I was gaining great knowledge and experience in the field of counseling. An interesting note about this program is that we actually started our clinical training by counseling with groups. This is quite different from most graduate psychology clinical programs, so it was yet another little evidence of things to come for me. I was once again more effective with groups than with individuals.

Perhaps the most enduring aspect of my graduate school experience was a personality typology system I learned, among the many others, today called Opposite Strengths. It became the topic of my dissertation research and has been a tool I've used in counseling and in coaching teams throughout my career. It helped me to personally improve a number of important relationships, and to know when some were not going to work out. There is a bit more about this tool in a later chapter. You can also see more about it at www.noblealignments.com. As you will see, it is clearly not the only personality tool that I use, but it has had significant impact on me through the years.

Journeyman Years

So how did I get from the ministry and counseling to corporate Organizational Effectiveness? Well, just like butterflies, which start out in one form, encounter a little transition period and then emerge as the true adult form they were born to be, a metamorphosis occurred in my life. I went through some personal discovery as I left the classroom and conducted my dissertation research. This discovery told me that church work was not in my future, that my career journey would be much broader in scope. I also could not stay married to Gary. I needed to let him go and be everything he could be as well.

So, off I went to see what I could learn and become. At this stage, I had no clue about "Organizational Effectiveness" and all that it involves. I did know that I liked working with groups, and the experience with Opposite Strengths gave me a taste of the world of corporate training. That would be my target.

I started out trying to sell training programs. I got introduced to a program helping sales people to overcome sales call reluctance. It was based in good behavioral psychology, something I did know about. But, I didn't know anything about sales, and I found I had my own call reluctance to deal with. Combined with many other emotional, spiritual, and practical changes in my life at that time, this was a really bad idea. I lasted about four months. Then, I tried selling Opposite Strengths to corporate training departments. That lasted less than six months as well. At least through that first year, I learned a little of what I did not know about selling, consulting, and the world outside a church organization. Today, I actually get to leverage that experience I thought was so bad, as I do now include some prospecting and sales training in my portfolio of services. It will actually be the focus of my next book!

Fortunately, I found a position with the City of Austin, where I could learn a variety of the fundamentals of organizational training and development. I didn't get the job because of my skills, but because I handled a group interview well! This turned out to be the true start of my 'journeyman' training in all aspects of what I now call 'Organizational Alchemy.' During these years, beginning with simply coordinating and brokering various training classes for city workers, I covered topics from garbage truck mechanics to sexual harassment prevention to national conferences and travel coordination. Over time, due to a very progressive city management, I taught and designed training programs in Total Quality Management, Facilitation Skills, and Manager/Supervisor skills. I was also privileged to work on some significant process improvements and organizational re-structuring. And, I led one major department through implementation of a dialogue-oriented performance management initiative.

This phase of my career certainly was not without some mistakes and mishaps, but I was very fortunate to have managers (Dixie, Ralph and Austan) who believed in me and gave me lots of freedom to take risks. I did embarrass them more than once. One time even got a nasty letter about how city funds were being used for what the critic saw as 'hokey' training, because of an experiential exercise we had created for process management. It wasn't perfect, I'll grant. Another time, a letter was sent to the department head, laughing at me, and him of course, regarding an article I'd written about change resilience. Yet, I was allowed to grow from those mistakes, and continue to try new things to help city workers improve themselves and their work. We did have some great successes, too, like a manager training for which one department funded some work on our facility to make it more useful! ALL those experiences were great lessons in being aware of broader impacts and organizational/political savvy, qualities we'll discuss briefly in the very last chapter of this book.

With those fundamental lessons and experiences, and a policy that allowed me to accrue vacation time over the years, I was able to go do some contract training at the Motorola sites located in Austin. Carol, with whom I had worked at the city, moved on to Motorola and introduced me to Jeanne-Marie, who then arranged for me to teach a three-day class every month. (Please see the Acknowledgements if you haven't already. These people deserve your attention!) I was able to teach those classes on vacation time for several months. Just as I was running out of vacation time, I was offered a permanent position there at Motorola. Like the opportunity at the City of Austin, this was life-changing, and the beginning of the next, most productive and important phase of my journeyman track to becoming a full-on Organizational Alchemist facilitating M.A.G.I.C. at work!

This phase was almost twelve years long, every year bringing new skills, practices, client relationships, HR partnerships and, yes, lessons learned. Jeanne-Marie was my manager and mentor through almost all of that time, literally walking with me through it all. She actually did take regular walks with me along Austin's hike-and-bike trail, around what is today called Lady Bird Lake. We called it simply Town Lake, back then. There is where I learned the value of conversation mastery, the M in the M.A.G.I.C. formula we'll go through in this book.

Just a few of the skills and practices I got to learn and exercise in those years included facilitating strategy development, organization design, large group work in process change, change management, new leader assimilation and integration, succession management, leadership assessment, performance rating and rankings assessment, spans and layers analysis and design, employee engagement, and corporate values development. We experienced the move of division headquarters from Phoenix to Austin, a major reorganization of the division, divestiture from Motorola to become a publicly traded entity, then purchase by venture capitalists to become privately owned. I worked with senior executives, functional leaders, engineering leaders and groups, and manufacturing managers.

Not only was all this enormous experience and learning for me in the US, but it also involved travel to Singapore, Malaysia, Australia, India, France, Germany, and Israel. It enabled me to see how people work in a very wide variety of physical, geographic, and cultural environments, and thus be able to further help them be more effective in their unique situations.

Through all those years, I kept a little picture of Merlin the Magician on my desk. I knew early on that we were providing a service to the organization that was a bit magical, and people were actually asking us to help in that way – to bring our "magic" to their teams and divisions. Today, I don't have that picture, but I do keep wands in my office, and have a great picture of Mickey the Wizard, from Fantasia, the Disney movie. Disney, himself a great magician, taught us that magic is really a discipline in the highest sense. So, in those Motorola days, the magic began to become clear, as I learned to exercise the discipline that is Organizational Alchemy (aka Organizational Development or Organizational Effectiveness).

Putting it all Together for Mastery

As more changed at Motorola and Freescale, the divestiture I stayed with, it became clear that I should continue my journey elsewhere. Jeanne-Marie had moved on, as had other of my closest work friends. I had good support from others, but it just became clear that it was time to go and grow in a new place. As before, in very timely way, an opportunity opened for me in a medical technologies company in Boulder, Colorado. This happened thanks to Sandra, who had been a HR executive at Motorola and Freescale and had moved on as well.

The company was headquartered in Massachusetts, and I became a corporate geek, supporting two businesses based in Colorado. In those early days, I was able to put to great use all my experience in talent management, facilitating succession planning, performance management, and leadership development. Later, I led an effort to develop global competencies models for sales reps and managers. Then, I led a global culture survey for one of the Boulder-based businesses. Finally, I led two very successful global engagement surveys for the corporation. When CEO leadership of the company changed, I was involved in a major effort to re-structure the organization, following a more center-led model. I became heavily involved in a cross-team intervention as the marketing strategy changed to include more digital channels. Finally, when it was announced the company would be acquired by an equally large and successful corporation, I became involved in the integration of the HR function and the development of a new, integrated set of leadership behavioral expectations.

It was in these seven years that I began to be able to say with confidence, "I know what I am doing." I am not naïve or arrogant enough to believe I know everything in the field, or to believe I am a master practitioner in every aspect of the field.

But I do believe I have achieved a level of mastery that should be shared with others.

When the opportunity presented itself I knew it was time to set off on my own, scary as that was then, and still is today. I felt the need to take my craft to others and to teach my own brand of Organizational Alchemy, called M.A.G.I.C.™

Chapter 2
The Foundations of Organizational Alchemy

To all my readers: This is a chapter you have my complete permission to skip if you want. It has some history in which only either mystics or professional Organizational Development types will have most interest. I'm a little on the "woo-woo" side in my life and work, and I'm grateful to those who have gone before me in this work. But I've spent enough time in business to know that many managers don't really care. They just want to know what works – not necessarily how it works. I found it completely fascinating, even inspiring, to look into the relationship between the ancient practice of alchemy and the more modern practice called "Organizational Effectiveness." I hope that you will see these connections too, but it is really okay if you don't. The rest of the book will be useful for you all the same!

Hermes, Alchemical Principles and Organizations

I don't know that much about mythology or the mystics. I just found that, as I got more experienced and capable in this whole field of Organizational Effectiveness, people began to view it as somehow magical, more art than science, and a bit miraculous. I began to see it a little that way myself! I don't know that others see me personally that way. But they do seem to see this work as both esoteric and practical. Therefore, I thought the use of terms like "alchemy" and even creating the M.A.G.I.C. acronym was cool and catchy in a slightly corny kind of way. Imagine my delight when I began to do some research and learned just how appropriate these terms actually are!

I won't pretend to have now become an authority on these things, but I do want to share a little of what I learned, so you can see how those of us (and YOU) who learn and exercise this work actually belong among the gods, mystics and magicians!

So first, I just looked at definitions of 'alchemy.' They all boil down to "the art of transformation."

Of course, many of the sources I read went into the ancient practice whereby alchemists supposedly were able to make gold from lead, and how alchemy was the pre-cursor to modern chemistry. But when you break it all down, the practices of traditional alchemy and Organizational Effectiveness (OE) are both about making change happen, sometimes achieving a complete metamorphosis, even the creation of something from nothing. You've heard of organizations "re-inventing" themselves, haven't you? And who doesn't love the stories of complete invention and innovation, like Apple, Amazon, and Google?

When I then looked into alchemy and the hermetic principles at its root, I thought of Hermes from Greek mythology and looked into him. Hermes is a god of transitions and boundaries, with a role as messenger and intercessor between mortals and the divine – *an ancient mythical facilitator!* The Roman adaptation of this god is also seen as the patron of commerce. Wow! No, I don't quite see my work as being a messenger from the divine, but I am a facilitator, sometimes interceding between seeming opposing parties! Transitions, boundaries, interceding, commerce, sometimes tricky......all fun stuff in the world of Organizational Effectiveness M.A.G.I.C.!

Looking deeper into alchemy, based on the hermetic principles, I was almost disappointed to find that the god Hermes (aka Thoth) was not the author, but instead they are ascribed to a medieval guy named Hermes Trismegistus ("Thrice Great"). Then I read that he actually influenced much of the Christian thinking and writing of the Reformation, and that the principles of alchemy very much apply to business and organizations, among many other things, and have already been applied in those arenas. So both the mythical character and the human mystic have encompassed the activities and root principles of Organizational Effectiveness, which I am now calling Organizational Alchemy.

I'll do my best here to provide a 'street' description of each principle, begging forgiveness of the real experts out there. I'll leave it to you to do a bit more study if you want to understand more. My purpose here is just to rationalize Organizational Alchemy as a magical process of its own.

The Sulfur Principle (Development). This whole principle suggests that everything in the universe strives toward perfection, moving from lower to high planes and effectively expressing the opposites in life. Development is the primary goal of what I'm now calling Organizational Alchemy. There is always room for change, for improvement in how leaders lead and how organizations achieve higher and higher aspirations, for dealing effectively with the conflicts and paradoxes that occur in the relationships, economics and operations of every business endeavor.

The Mercury Principle (Vision). This principle emphasizes the power of the mind and imagination to create and to effect change. In the more mundane world of business and organizations, we might call that 'vision.' Further, the principle suggests that whatever the mind creates emerges with a sort of reflection of the creator, a signature of sorts. In marketing, we would call that 'branding.' In the world of Organizational Alchemy, I would suggest that the mental state of the practitioner has impact on the client, and the 'group mind' has much to do with how successful will be the results of any intervention. There is a technique known as Appreciative Inquiry, which begins with that mental imagining of what can be. The best change management frameworks also begin with a vision of what better future the change will bring.

The Salt Principle (Results). Manifestation is the more esoteric word the mystics use here. This principle speaks to the complex processing that occurs to achieve a new metamorphosis, whether that is the physical or non-physical realm. In my own career and life, I have experience metamorphoses of many sorts, as you may have read in that lengthy first chapter. When we see the successful outcomes of a process as simple as a new manager assimilation, or as complex as a major acquisition or divestiture, it does look like something magical has occurred.

Early Organizational Alchemists

I can't refer to any mythical gods, but M.A.G.I.C.™ has some heroes of its own. While they never used this term, nor did I ever read in their books reference to sulfur, mercury and salt, there are many who created and contributed to the discipline of Organizational Development/Effectiveness, and what I now call Organizational Alchemy. They ALL discuss change and transformation, development, vision, and results.

Frederick Taylor is where most of us understand the beginning of our craft. He has been called the father of "Scientific Management," but he should be given more credit than most allow for his views of the power of motivation. Douglas McGregor gave more clarity to motivation and leadership. Kurt Lewin, Edgar Schein, and Daniel Denison gave us more clarity around organizational culture and change. Marvin Weisbord, among others, taught us new ways to effect change in organizations, with large group processes and practices. Jay Galbraith, Ed Lawler and David Nadler gave us great organization design methods and frameworks. Peter Senge brought us the "learning organization." And the folks at McKinsey consulting gave us the '7s model' – strategy, structure, systems, style, staff, skills, shared values.

...and then there is M.A.G.I.C.™

Given this background and a legacy of many who've come before me, I have nothing really brand new to offer here. What I'm proposing here is something very similar to what these masters have given us, and something just a little different. I've tried to provide a basic synthesis of all these, giving attention to strategic, structural and people-focused processes and practices involved in organizational effectiveness and change. And, hopefully, you'll find it memorable.

Before I describe the acronym in more detail, let's talk very briefly about the graphic. First, I've chosen overlapping diamond shapes to represent the connections that are part of every aspect of Organizational Alchemy. The gemstones at these intersections represent not only the value of these connections, but there is also metaphysical meaning behind the particular gem colors used in the color version -- Sapphire and Ruby:

Ruby is often referred to as a symbol of a clear mind, increased concentration and motivation, and brings a sense of power to the wearer, a self-confidence and determination that overcomes timidity and propels one toward prosperity and achievement. Good things for a leader and organization to have, right?

Sapphire is said to bring order and healing to the mind, lending strength and focus, and an ability to see beneath surface appearances to underlying truths and to utilize that knowledge. It stimulates access to deeper levels of consciousness in order to gain a fuller understanding. Blue Sapphire embraces order, structure, and self-discipline, and is ideal for accomplishing goals and manifesting ideas into physical form. Sounds a lot like the focus of M.A.G.I.C., both in its disciplined exercise and in the qualities and mindset required of the leader or consultant working it.

Let's take the high level view at how M.A.G.I.C. provides the structure for Organizational Alchemy.

M – Master Conversations for Peak Performance. Effective organizations depend on the top performance of the people within them. Too often, leaders, managers and employees do not know how to have the kinds of conversations that will provide the clarity, recognition, feedback, and development coaching to ensure the very best work of everyone.

A – Align Goals, Roles, and Teams. Misalignment, often resulting from poor or non-existent conversations, is the primary reason that organizations cannot achieve what they really want to. In my experience, most of what my clients have seen as something magical was simply the act of getting people in the room to get aligned on what they were trying to accomplish, who was doing what in the process, and how they stay coordinated and productive as a team.

G – Grow Talent and Leadership. Some have said that talent is over-rated, and talent alone is not the formula for great organizations. What I have seen, however, is that without the right talent, and the leadership to guide them to a common vision, no amount of talk, coordination, enthusiasm, adaptability or effort can make an organization world-class. It is no wonder that 'G' here is at the very center of M.A.G.I.C.

I – Ignite Active Engagement. A warm room on a cold day executes on a key goal – to avoid hypothermia. However, if the room has a burning fireplace, the room takes on a whole new dimension. It seems to encourage the inhabitants to gather around it and engage with each other in activity that creates connection and energy. So it is in business organizations. Execution to plan happens all the time, but when the added dimension of an environment that gets everyone's complete attention, to the task and to each other, working groups become teams and businesses are transformed into coveted places to spend careers. They become those teams that have accomplished tremendous goals, and then want to work with each other again towards the next, even bigger vision.

C – Change Readily – well T.I.M.E.D. One thing is certain -- nothing stays the same. If we are growing, we are changing. Business organizations today are changing more frequently and dramatically than ever before. The temptation can be to simply make changes as a matter of habit, rather than as a response to environmental, strategic, technical or other influences. Change too early or too quickly, without ensuring all stakeholders are engaged, can be a recipe for the wheels falling off the proverbial bus. Change too slowly or too late and the organization faces the potential of 'death by a thousand cuts.' Adeptness not only at the mechanics of change, but also at the human and business readiness for change is now a fundamental requirement for sustained success in today's corporate environments.

Okay, you have PLENTY of background and context, now let's get to it!

Chapter 3
Master Conversations for Peak Performance

In business, we all succeed or fail with and through other people. If we are solo-preneurs, our team may be a collection of those who support our efforts, such as the attorney, the accountant, the IT professional, the printer, and so on. If your organization is growing, you may have a small team of people whom you pay for their support to your business. If you are a large enterprise, you may have whole departments executing to the strategies and goals of the business. In all cases, in order to get the very best from these teams, conversation is necessary. Not just any conversation – clear, open conversations that ensure people both know how to perform their best, and want to do that for you. Yes, I'm talking about the annual Performance Review – but I'm also talking about much, much more.

From my viewpoint, the two primary qualities of conversation that must always be present in order to achieve the results you want are, as stated above, clarity and openness. Let's look at these individually:

CLARITY

When you look through clear glass, water, cellophane or lucite, you see what is on the other side of it. Looking at your toes in a clear swimming pool or clear ocean at the beach, all the distinctions between them are apparent to you. There is no fuzziness. You don't mistake your own toes for those of someone else. You don't mistake them for your fingers. Such is the case in clear conversation. Parties on either side of the discussion experience no ambiguity or indistinctness of the topic, expectations, or desired outcomes. There is no room for error.

So to master the conversations that get the performance you want, master clarity. What is your main point? State it clearly and in the beginning of the conversation. Especially in sensitive or uncomfortable conversations, many leaders tend to hesitate and talk around the main topic rather than speak directly about the situation. If you are unclear about your point, people will be confused, and confused minds accomplish nothing.

Clarity does not mean you have to use lots of words. That often only adds to the ambiguity. Clarity is specific, but not highly detailed. Say exactly what you want or what you intend. Ask the other(s) in the conversation to use their own words to test their understanding of what you are requesting.

Generalizing, or worse, name-calling, is not clarity. Comments like "You're the best" or "You're a loser," are not clear. They are opinions. Be specific about what you like or don't like…what exactly you want, or what exactly you do not want.

In organizations, no matter how small or large, it is so easy to get messages crossed. Most Performance Management processes are originally designed to ensure clarity about goals, goal achievement and the evaluation of the results achieved. They were never designed, however, to replace the actual conversation necessary for full clarity.

OPENNESS

Thesaurus entries for the word "openness" include terms such as receptivity, impartiality, observance, interest, acceptance, understanding. Mastering business conversations, therefore, requires all parties to *suspend judgment*. This may be even more difficult than the quality of clarity discussed above. We all bring to work our own histories, personalities, values, and expectations, which can cause us to make snap judgments and cloud our ability to understand the communications and intents of others.

To maintain a position of impartiality, or objective observation, allows all parties the freedom to speak more honestly and experience a greater sense of being understood, which then allows for more trust in the relationship, and more creative problem solving, which in turn results in higher performance levels.

With these two qualities of clarity and openness, the following types of conversations become much more efficient, productive and result in top performance.

Tough Conversations

I'm hitting this right up front, because let's face it -- this is what we all have the most trouble with. It somehow seems so much easier to have productive conversations when things are going well, when parties in the conversation "get" each other. The problems occur when one or more in the situation are not getting what they want. In fact, many companies spend enormous amounts of time, energy and money on well-engineered processes and slick technologies for managing performance, and still don't get the outcomes they seek because managers just don't want to have the tough conversations necessary to ensure employees are clear about the expectations of them, and about what went wrong when things did not go as expected.

The truth, however, is that tough conversations don't have to be tough most of the time. The secret? *Have conversations more often.* Yep, that takes a little time and attention – but not as much as when you have waited until results are so poor they have cost the company money and the conversation you now have to have creates a bit of drama and perhaps turnover costs. Here's the 'path' of a conversation that is more corrective than all-out tough, as long as it happens when you first see something going wrong. I'm using the acronym N.A.A.N. I don't personally like Indian food, but who doesn't love naan bread?

Notice – Invite your employee or supplier into a conversation. Make them aware of your concern by simply commenting that you notice a particular performance challenge or unproductive behavior. Be very clear and specific about what you notice. Have this conversation as near the occurrence of the error or behavior as possible, to avoid confusion or escalation of undesired results.

Ask -- Ask the person about the performance or behavior. How do they see it? What happened? What do they think needs to happen to improve? Seek to truly understand. Stay open, even if the other person reacts defensively.

Adjust – Agree on a plan to adjust and correct in the future. Commit to the plan, including when you will discuss progress.

Notice – At the time allotted, or as soon as you notice improved performance or behavior, note your observation to the employee or supplier. Celebrate if the adjustment had positive results. If things have not changed, discuss obstacles and the plan going forward, including the consequences of continued non-performance.

If you don't have these NAAN conversations early, when you see a pattern but before things have escalated, you'll be forced into the tough conversations, which are longer, more intense and often emotional. And if you don't have those, the rest of these conversations discussed will not be possible. For more articles and references regarding these difficult situations, check out my website at www.noblealignments.com.

Development Conversations

These are much more fun to have than the corrective or tough ones, because they speak to how you help others grow, particularly those directly employed by you. Development conversations speak to both the strengths and the learning opportunities your employee(s) have. The tools used for these conversations can be quite simple, or very sophisticated. The process goes basically like this:

1. *Identify* the capabilities/skills most important to accomplish the role the employee is assigned to fulfill. This can be done simply by brainstorming 5-10 key capabilities required, as tactical as "Mastery of MS Office," or as behavioral as "Manages Matrix Relationships." You can also check with your professional association. Many have already developed robust models of competence in their field. Or, you can conduct a much more sophisticated study, typically facilitated by a consultant to outline the core competencies required.

2. *Assess* your employee against each capability/skill, using your own observations and getting feedback from others. You can do this via email survey of those who work with your employee, a series of interviews conducted by you or some outside party, or a well-researched 360-feedback survey.

3. *Review* the results of your assessment, highlighting the 1-3 areas where your employee has greatest strength, and the 1-3 areas you most want her/him to work to improve. The bottom line here is always a conversation, regardless of the tools used to bring you here.

   a. Strengths first – with discussion of how to leverage them (lunch-n-learns, partnering with peers, presenting at a conference, etc.)
   b. Learning opportunities – with discussion of how to strengthen.

4. *Plan* for the next 6-18 months. How will you leverage this employee's strengths, for his/her own continued development and performance and for that of the rest of the team (including you!)? What experiences, education, and or coaching will help your employee strengthen those areas you have identified as most critical to his/her continued success and growth on the job? Be careful here not to depend on books, webinars or other training/educational solutions alone. There is high value in these opportunities, but the research says that the most lasting change happens with experiences that require actually practicing the capabilities you are focusing on. Next to that is coaching, THEN the educational stuff.

   a. Don't do all the work for your employee, and don't make him/her do all the work. Help by providing a few

potential resources or people to talk to. Your primary
role is facilitator/guide, less teacher/parent.
b. Include quarterly check-in discussions in the plan, for
review of BOTH kinds of development activity.

Development conversations are NOT corrective/tough
conversations. They are the conversations that allow you and
your employees(s) to raise the capability and performance of the
team, thus increasing the results you achieve as a team,
department or enterprise. The big secret here is that mastery of
development conversations often leads to employee loyalty,
high levels of engagement, excellent performance. You may also
get a reputation as a great manager people want to work for!

Development conversations are easier with your top performers,
and those should be your top priority people for such
conversations. However, EVERY employee should have the
opportunity to understand and use fully their strengths, and to
understand and develop those areas where they are not so
strong. It is more than possible for marginal employees to
become good ones, and for good ones to become GREAT. For
the less effective employees, this conversation allows you and
them to see what is possible, and to focus on things other than
the corrective conversations you may have been having. The
development conversation is a must-do with everyone on your
team.

In fact, you should have development conversations with the
team as a whole, in addition to the individual conversations.
Pull all the results of your assessments together and show the
team a report of their combined strengths and learning
opportunities. Create a learning plan together!

Check out my website, www.noblealignments.com, for development planning tools and templates.

Career Conversations

Managers sometimes shy away from these, thinking they are not "career counselors," but there is no need for fear. These can be some of the most rewarding and fun for both employee and manager! I see four things you need in order to have such a conversation:

- Openness to listen to what the employee dreams about and believes he/she is capable of
- Understanding a bit about what the company/industry needs in the future
- Honesty (sometime brutal) about what you observe as the employee's capabilities and potential
- Willingness to help your employee identify and talk with others who may have the roles to which he/she is aspiring

Unlike development conversations, reserve career conversations for the top 5-10% of your employees, with perhaps a few exceptions. Yes, everyone has concerns about the direction of their career and should have the right to seek their bliss. However, your time, and the investment of the company, is best spent on those topmost employees whom you want to keep and grow to become leaders in the enterprise.

I'm not saying you "brush off" employees who ask you about their future with the company, their unique contribution, etc. Many of these questions may be addressed during regular development conversations, and the rest can be addressed by some of the great tools out on the market today for people to drive their own careers. I do believe companies should provide a few of those tools, or at least show employees how to get to them.

What I'm talking about is when *you* should be the *initiator* of conversations about career.

There are those who disagree with me on this, but my opinion is that top performers and high potential employees should know their status. I believe these people are more frequently very high achievers who are very hard on themselves and do not typically hold attitudes of entitlement when they learn of their status. More often, it simply motivates them to give even more of themselves to the cause of the organization and earn the places of leadership they hope to gain.

The challenges to this philosophy come when managers do not adhere to the 4 main requirements of good career conversations noted above. If they are not honest with these achievers about their strengths and opportunities, disappointment is probable. I have seen highly professional, great performers who were told of their potential be very disappointed when the promotions or new opportunities did not materialize because managers had not been open, and perhaps even brutally honest, about all the employee needed to achieve. More frequently, I have seen people disappointed because neither they, nor their manager, had gotten very clear about what the employee truly wants and what the company needs going forward. Even more frequently, the employee and manager had not done the work of getting the employee in front of others who could help them grow in their own roles and then into the next. They did not help the employee get the kind of exposure and sponsorship necessary to ensure every opportunity to move into desired career roles.

Performance Conversations

Every manager I have ever worked with has hated this term, "Performance Management." It typically makes them think of the annual exercise that takes almost a full business quarter, includes a lot of administrative drudgery and ends in conversations with employees about why their pay is not what they want it to be. So, I'm not going to make this entirely about that process.

What I am going to talk about here is the intent of those processes – the conversation. Yep – another conversation.

Performance conversations should not happen just once a year. Maybe that is the answer. Just like development conversations, they should happen frequently, for the best and the worst performers, and for everyone in the middle. We do the formal process every year for multiple reasons, including ensuring that we have protected ourselves in the rare event that someone is disgruntled enough to file a lawsuit. We also conduct the formal Performance Management process to be sure we have documented a history of the employee's performance for his/her future managers to understand. And, we conduct that formal process, truthfully, to be sure everyone gets SOMETHING. Maybe not you, but there are too many managers who do not let their employees know how they are doing – ever. Then, these same managers act surprised when their best employees leave, or when a poor employee gets angry about getting low or no pay increases, is passed over for desirable projects or promotions, or is placed on notice that his/her job is in jeopardy if performance doesn't improve.

Nothing can replace regular performance conversations, regardless of the sophistication of your system. Today, there is growing popularity of completely doing away with these systems. However, before you throw out your current process/system, be sure you master conversations!

Without a few "teeth," great conversations may not be enough. When I first began working in this field, I was in municipal government, where there was an active association of employees who protected workers, perhaps a bit too much. It was very hard to make a case to remove an under-performing or consistently misbehaving employee. Additionally, city budgets made it difficult to provide much of a pay increase or other rewards to strong performers. Thus, our Performance Management process, while robust, was difficult to execute. Managers struggled to see the point.

When I moved into the corporate sector, the issues we faced in the municipality were gone, but we still struggled to ensure that performance conversations were regular, honest, and consistent with decisions made about the employee's pay, development, and continued employment. We would see years where the business was not performing well at all, compared to the market/industry, yet more than seventy percent of our employees (and managers) received high performance ratings. How could that be? Then, when we either made promotion or workforce reduction decisions, those selected (or not) could not distinguish why they were selected versus their peers.

So what happened next? You probably guessed – forced ranking! We created a new rating scale, then imposed on all parts of the organization a distribution of those ratings. We taught all managers a process for calibrating with each other on the meaning of the ratings, so one manager's "Exceeds" was not another manager's "Meets." I facilitated many of those meetings, where managers struggled to give a good employee a lesser rating, sometimes just because that employee had not made him/herself known to the other managers in the calibration session. Those in the lowest category were put on improvement plans or laid off, raising the performance bar further for the next round.

There is absolutely nothing wrong with raising the bar for performance. Every company must do that just to stay in business, much less grow. But, by using this methodology, it became challenging to try to build a culture of collaboration and innovation when everyone was competing for the right ratings, or at least to stay out of the wrong ones!

Am I saying that performance conversations and formal Performance Management processes should not ever include annual ratings? Maybe – maybe not. The answer to that really depends on the company, its strategy and maturity, and more importantly, how well managers are trained in the skills of good management conversations. If you are questioning what your company should do, get some help thinking through that. For a little more around this issue, check out my website at www.noblealignments.com.

Whether you have a rating/ranking system, or you don't, master the performance conversation!

Here's a brief outline of what that conversation should include:

1. Set Goals. In most professional situations, the employee and the manager should work together to create performance goals for a specified period of time. This is often a year, but in many situations 6 months may be more appropriate. In some cases, such as in R&D, the goals are longer term, but should be broken into more manageable sub-goals or process steps, in order to review progress and adjust if necessary.

2. Review the list of goals you and the employee have established for him/her for the performance period.
3. Agree on a meeting time when you both will bring comments and evidence to show how he/she has progressed (or not) on each goal.
4. The employee speaks to specific accomplishments and to obstacles faced, where he/she is confident the goal will be achieved, where help is needed, where the goal may need to be re-negotiated.
5. You bring your own thoughts regarding each goal. Provide the recognition or coaching where appropriate, and adjust goals where necessary.
6. You each state your perception of the employee's overall performance, and discuss key development needs and opportunities.
7. Commit to the assessment, and to the adjusted goals, establishing when you will meet next to evaluate progress.

This should all be documented, whether in a sophisticated system or in a desk folder. This ensures you are both clear on the agreements, not to mention any legal protections, should they become necessary.

Coaching Conversations

I'm going to be quick here, because the kind of conversation I'm talking about here should be quick. These conversations are slightly different from the others, as they are often "in the moment," more casual and very specific to a single behavior or performance incident. They can be either a reinforcement of something well done, or a quick correction of a single error (not a pattern – save that for a NAAN conversation).

Perhaps the thing to remember here is timing.

When you want to recognize and reinforce something well done, communicate that immediately after you notice it. Give a quick congratulations in person, on the phone or in a quick email, text or voice mail. Just be sure to be specific about exactly what the person did to receive the kudo. Was the presentation given in exactly the time allotted? Was the project plan thorough and clear? Was an assignment delivered early and with some added helpful features? Whatever, just a little reinforcement makes a difference. No response from the employee is necessary...just your genuine gratitude for their contribution.

When you want to correct some error or minor incident before it becomes a pattern, or simply to help someone improve on already good performance, make it quick and typically just before they do that task the next time. This helps them pay attention more closely. Were there typos? Ask them to do a quick spell check or have someone proofread for them before submitting. Was the presentation too long? Have them practice with a timer before the next one. It is important here to either suggest a plan for avoiding the error the next time, or to elicit that plan from the employee.

Coaching doesn't need to be "nagging," nor should it be "micro-managing." It should also not be high praise for the tiniest achievements. This kind of conversation should be delivered with the attitude that you appreciate the employee and you are simply offering help for continuous improvement. They should all have the tone of little "emotional deposits" that build the employee's confidence and skill.

1-on-1 Conversations

To ensure conversations are frequent enough to ensure top performance and to avoid surprises during any of the other conversations, I always recommend that managers have regularly scheduled 1-on-1 conversations with their employees. These can be half-hour discussions with the same structure every time, or they can vary in length and structure to match the requirements of the function and ongoing projects and goals.

It is easy to let busy meeting, travel and other schedule requirements take priority over these conversations, which sometimes seem lower priority than other more urgent matters. That is actually the beauty of these conversations. The more disciplined you are at conducting these, the fewer truly urgent matters you have to deal with.

The regular 1-on-1 can focus on any of the other types of conversations, as well as be a forum for regular progress reviews. Here's a brief list of potential components to include:

- Project updates
- Development progress
- Communication of key organizational plans or changes
- NAAN discussions
- Short-term targeted activities/goals
- Problem solving/help needed

Team Conversations

Last, but soooooo not least in this list of conversations to master for top performance is the team conversation. For me, this is the most fun kind of conversation to talk about and to have. I'm not yet talking about team-building here. That is in the next chapter. Great team conversations should result in innovations in product or process, in clear agreements and plans for execution to team goals, and in higher levels of team cohesion to perform at greater levels.

I'm talking here about team brainstorming and about good team meetings management:

BRAINSTORMING – the stuff of creativity. Nothing was ever created without a thought in someone's mind at some point. So brainstorming is the practice of just letting out of your mind whatever is in there so something new can be created or at least improved. There are many ways to brainstorm, and typically brainstorming in a group is the best way. The ideas of many, even when executed by one, are much more creative than if any one member of the group tried to create on their own. There are great ways to brainstorm on your own as well, but this is about team conversations, so let's stick with that. Here are just a few methods for the team to use when brainstorming:

Nominal Group Technique – This is a way to distill down a number of ideas into those few the group wants to further develop. The process involves groups members assigning a rank order to the ideas presented (1st, 2nd, 3rd, etc.), then the votes are tallied. Those ideas gaining the most votes are then considered for another round of discussion and development. There are lots of variations to this technique, but the basic concept is one of voting. I'm personally fond of giving participants a little supply of sticky "dots" (small round labels/stickers) and allowing them to place the dots on a flip chart beside the ideas they most want considered.

Group Idea Passing – This method allows for more detailed development of each idea more thoroughly. It starts with each person writing an idea, or adding to an idea presented by the facilitator. Then, ideas are passed to the next person in the group, for that next person to add to what has already been offered regarding that particular idea. The passing stops when ideas land back in the hands of the original contributor. Again, there can be multiple variations, but the concept is that of developing each idea more thoroughly before it is openly discussed with the rest of the team.

Team Idea Mapping – This one involves a bit more visual stimulation for the team. The two main ways this happens is through "affinity diagram" or a group "mind map."

In the *affinity diagram*, team members brainstorm all their ideas related to the problem presented on little self-stick notes, one idea per note paper. Then, they all put their papers up on the wall or large chart paper. Silently, they review all the ideas and then begin to put them into related categories. They then discuss the titles of the categories and observe things like how many ideas were related to one category over another, what ideas were very similar or exactly like others, and so forth. The discussion can then move to what categories should be the focus of the team's attention for further development and execution planning.

In the *group mind map*, the central problem is written in a circle in the middle of a large sheet of chart paper or on a large whiteboard. As team members have ideas, branches can be drawn with the ideas written at the end of the branch. Then, to develop ideas further, smaller branches can be drawn off the original branches, and so forth. The final picture may be a bit messy, but the team gains a sense how ideas are related to each other and are able to discuss thoroughly the possibilities and limitations of the ideas on the board.

All these methods can be easily learned, and I recommend that all managers learn how to lead such discussions. In fact, I recommend that everyone learn how to brainstorm and how to facilitate a brainstorming session. Start with a simple process and get more creative with that.

Fundamental rules when brainstorming:
- Be clear about the objective of a brainstorming session: develop one idea? Solve a problem? Streamline a process? Identify a new product or features? Decide on a location for the sales meeting? The possibilities are endless.
- Defer judgment on any idea – discourage members from dismissing any ideas they believe are not good.
- Get as many ideas out as possible – start with quantity, then use the methods above to get at quality
- Crazy ideas can lead to. the best solutions – don't immediately dismiss wild ideas – get them "on the table."
- Combine ideas. Build on others presented. Creativity is sometimes a single insight, sometimes the cumulative result of the group's insights.

MEETINGS MANAGEMENT – the bane of business life if not done well, very energizing and productive if mastered. Everything we do requires meetings of some sort, whether planning the next family vacation (even if you are single!), solving daily business problems, or building the vision and strategy for the company's next level of growth. Meetings can include you, yourself and you – or they can be massive, including hundreds to thousands of people.

The problem with most meetings is that little or no thought has been put into the purpose of the meeting, the outcomes expected at the end of the meeting, the time required to achieve the outcomes, or the appropriate participants required. So let's look at some basics of meeting design first. A good meeting should include the following components.

Purpose – WHY are you meeting? What is the general purpose of this meeting? Weekly briefing? Information? Planning? Decision? Celebration? What is the main reason you are bringing this particular group of people together to do?

Desired Outcomes – WHAT do you want to leave the meeting having accomplished? There could be several of these for any meeting. The important thing to remember here is the more objectives you have, the longer your meeting is likely to be. Outlining the specific outcomes you want to leave the meeting with will help you decide if it is one meeting or more, a few people or many, a 10 minute stand-up meeting or a 3-day working session.

Participants – WHO should attend the meeting, and who can you not have the meeting without their presence and active participation? Who should NOT be in the meeting, and why? How many participants should be there, and why? What will be the role of each participant in the meeting? Do they simply need to be informed? Do they need to decide on something? Do they need to contribute to a new idea, or plan, or process? What do you want these carefully selected participants to DO?

Preliminary Materials/Prep – HOW should participants (including you, the leader) prepare for this meeting? What kinds of materials will they need to read, prepare, and/or send before the meeting? What materials do you need to send them?

Tentative Agenda – I say "tentative" because most agendas change somehow as the meeting progresses. The topics, the timing, or other aspects of the agenda may require adjustment as the discussions go on. There is a fragile balance to maneuver here. This is where the bulk of meeting MANAGEMENT comes in. While agendas are made to be adjusted, be cautious of some meeting behaviors that may prolong the discussions unnecessarily. We'll talk about that shortly. Back to your agenda.

The various topics on your agenda should map back to your objectives and desired outcomes. Carefully assign the time you think each topic will require first. Don't just try to make all the topics fit into the time you have allotted (or been given) for the meeting. This step helps you understand whether you need a meeting at all, more meetings, a longer meeting, or even separate working meetings for certain topics. If deciding between 4 colors for your new office carpet will take 1 hour because you are all decorators and, therefore, very selective, don't put anything else on the agenda for a 1-hour meeting. Conversely, don't plan a 1-hour meeting when you just need 10 minutes to make an announcement about the date for the next employee picnic.

Once you have assigned the time necessary for each item in the agenda, organize the topics in a way that makes sense. The most critical items should be first on the agenda, ensuring you take care of the most important business in case you don't get through all items. The logic of the agenda is important too. Let like items be dealt with together. You may actually be able to save a bit of time this way. Check out the website for a couple of simple agenda planning templates: www.noblealignments.com

Now, a little about MANAGING the meeting you have so carefully designed. Watch for and tactfully discourage time-wasting or even destructive behaviors. There are many books and resources out there to help with this. I recommend most of them. To name a few of those behaviors here, though:

- Tardiness – don't wait for all the participants to start the meeting. Many teams actually have a "late payment," anywhere from $1-100 per minute, depending on the group, to impose on latecomers. This not only cures the habit, but also builds the fund for the next team outing or favorite charity.

- Over-participating/Dominance – Limit pontificators to 3 minutes, and 3 opportunities to speak during the course of the meeting. After that, if they really have something they must say, expand the purpose of the late payment jar to that of a speech jar, charging a hefty amount per minute extra.
- Under-participation – This is sometimes in reaction to, or even passive aggression against the dominator/over-participator. Set the pattern of being unafraid of silence, even halting someone from speaking up a second or third time in order to give time and space for others to think before they offer their responses.
- PA non-verbals – Passive aggression (PA) is a killer for team conversations. Have a coaching or NAAN conversation with participants you observe doing this. Eye rolls, head shakes, inappropriate laughter, jaw clenching, hiding in text or email messaging, or more obvious signals have no place in a meeting where productivity is imperative. If you need to, keep of little private "tic sheet" to tally when you see this happening, so you have some data when you have the talk with offenders. See the next chapter, in the 'Team Effectiveness' section, for guidance if this is revealing some conflict that needs addressed.

There are many more behaviors that could be identified. And, there are a number of positive ones you should reinforce. Let's leave this for now, though. The website has some tools for meeting behaviors you should check out. www.noblealignments.com

So, that's it for Mastering Conversations for Top Performance. These conversations will be fundamental to all the other areas in this M.A.G.I.C. model. Mobilizing people starts with talking to them.

Let's move on to Align Goals, Roles, and Teams, the fundamental operating system of getting things done in business.

Chapter 4
Align Goals, Roles and Teams

Here is a little assignment for you. Go to the internet and search for "alignment." You'll first find many ads for wheel alignments for your vehicle. Then, you'll find references to alignment as a means of character development in the Dungeons and Dragons game. Searching Amazon.com for the word will lead you to books regarding orthopedic and skeletal alignment. Searching for 'business alignment' can bring up multiple definitions and methodologies, all intended at a similar outcome.

To align anything means to arrange, coordinate, organize, or adjust.

When a car gets out of alignment, it is difficult to steer it where you want it to go, not to mention the wear and tear on your tires. In like manner, companies who get out of alignment don't achieve what they intend, and there is much wear and tear on their people!

Alignment – Horizontal, Vertical, Global

Before we get into specifics of aligning goals, roles, and teams, as the chapter title promises, let's look at the various directions of alignment in organizations.

Horizontal Alignment is critical in every organization, large or small. This has to do with ensuring everyone is coordinated across all functions or departments, and in larger organizations, across business units. Everyone needs to be at least aware of what the others are doing. More importantly, everyone needs to understand how their goals and activities impact everyone else, how the handoffs need to work, where there is creative tension versus where there is unproductive conflict. While this seems logical, the larger the organization, the harder this is to achieve smoothly. This is where bureaucracies and complex governance systems get created.

Horizontal alignment (or lack thereof) happens across independent businesses or organizations as well. Consider the medical world. There exist some multi-disciplinary practices, but often the task of aligning care across multiple specialists, not to mention insurance, pharmaceutical and home care suppliers can become a serious exercise in frustration. Yet, it is a critical, often life-dependent exercise.

Vertical Alignment is something that seems a bit more natural to us. This is the coordination up and down the hierarchy, internal to a department, function or business unit, between managers and their teams. When aligned, the group operates smoothly, people get along, and goals are met and even exceeded. When misaligned, there is confusion, conflict, and poor results.

Global Alignment is the most complex of the three alignments to address in business. Essentially, it is another layer of horizontal alignment, albeit a complicated one. This has to do with getting coordinated across geographic boundaries and characteristics. Not only are there cultural and language differences that must be addressed, but a very complex web of country-to-country laws and practices regarding commerce, human resources, currencies, quality and regulatory requirements, and more. Small companies hoping to expand globally are faced with learning whole new skillsets as they seek to build cooperative and profitable relationships across global boundaries. Large multinational companies spend heavily in time, energy and money on the continuing effort to stay aligned across global entities.

Sound overwhelming? It can be. However, there is a practice called "Organization Design" that helps to break this whole effort down into manageable pieces. And you start with aligning everyone on the goals, getting clear on roles, and ensuring teams are effective. With these in motion, THEN you deal with the more complex issues.

So let's get started.

Strategy and Goal Alignment

If I were to ask each person in your organization their picture of what greatness will look like for your business, I expect I would get almost as many varying answers as the number of people asked….that is, unless you have already mastered alignment. How can we expect to mobilize people toward greatness if they all have a different direction in their own minds? The purpose and value in organizations is that they are built to achieve common, or at least aligned, vision, strategies and goals!

Therefore, the first task in getting aligned on strategies and goals is to create them. There are many, many ways to go about this, and my intent, at least in this particular book, is not to go through the process of strategy development in detail, as it is to emphasize alignment. I'll very briefly go over some key points regarding strategy and goal development here:

Vision. There's that word (remember Mercury from chapter 2). If you really want a powerful organization, you'll need to draw that picture for each other. You don't have to envision world dominance in your field, although you could, but you will need to work on what greatness really does mean for you, your particular business. If you run a car wash, is your vision "a clean car for everyone in the city/state/country?" It can be that simple and specific, or much more ambitious and broad. Consider Amazon's vision to be "earth's most customer centric company, to build a place where people can come to find and discover anything they might want to buy online." The important thing about a vision is that it reflect a BIG dream you have. Greatness begins with a thought, a mental picture.

Strategy. Don't "boil the ocean" here with ambitions too big to accomplish in reasonable times. The way to think about strategy is to consider, in big chunks, how you will go about achieving your vision. In the car wash example, your strategy may include a franchise strategy, cleaning products manufacture and marketing, even a customer education strategy. These would be considered parts of your overall business model.

Additionally, you may need to include a competitive strategy, a growth strategy, and talent/people strategy, and others that support your business model/strategy. Whatever your key strategies, it is important that you and your senior leaders, at the very least, align on these. This doesn't mean there won't be a little tension, which may actually be very creative. Again consider the car wash. Let's say your facilities leader promotes a maintenance strategy for long-term sustainability of machines and highest quality of cleaning for the vehicles, but your sales/marketing leader promotes a strategy for 24-7 operating hours. One is seeking optimal revenue while the other is seeking cost efficiencies and quality standards. The work of negotiating through this tension can result in a creative solution that meets both objectives.

I recommend a few strategies, five at most, then rank those in priority order.

Annual Goals. Here, think in terms of Priorities, Objectives (Intentions), and Success Indicators (Numbers). This is where alignment becomes most critical, but very difficult to achieve if the vision and strategy are not already in alignment. Many businesses make the mistake of developing only their annual goals and priorities without really understanding what they are trying to accomplish longer term.

Assuming you have done the work of vision and strategy, it is often helpful to start 3 years out, then back into the next year. For each of your key strategies, identify 3-5 goals to be accomplished in the next 3 years. Then for each goal, set your intended objective for year 3, 2 and the coming year. These objectives should be stated as specifically as possible, with a way to measure your success or failure to meet them. If you want 3 new locations by end of year 3, for each year, you'll need sales and finance goals to ensure funding, talent goals to ensure management and staffing, facilities and real estate goals to ensure the space, buildings and equipment are ready. And everyone will need to be aligned across and down the organization to be sure you all arrive at the same place every year.

What if your facility is built, the cars are lining up, but the equipment never got connected to all the power/water supplies. The stories exist, even in very large organizations, where the manufacturing facility was built, the products were designed, but the equipment was not ordered and installed in time to meet production deadlines. Imagine how much this costs in customer satisfaction and lost sales! Yes, this has to do with good project planning. But a great project plan starts with aligned goals.

Across, then down. As you set goals, ensure there is alignment across the team, both horizontally and globally, before you ask them to then work with their teams to set their goals. You can do this in a very cascaded fashion, communicating the larger organizational goals, then department goals, then building individual goals. Another way to accomplish this is through a large group event. This won't work for every business, but in companies of enough scale can involve people from every level in a meeting where everyone has input into getting all the goals and objectives lined up in a way that is achievable. This builds engagement and commitment among your employees, not to mention ensuring you have considered the many 'front line' issues that need addressed as you set your plans. After the event, employees are more comfortable accomplishing personal goals, as they participated in aligning everything across the organization. They are less likely to get confused about what is expected of them, versus others on the team or organization.

Alignment isn't annual--it is ongoing. Yes, annual is the place to start, but things change quickly in business today, so plan for regular alignment reviews. This can happen as part of your regular business reviews. If you don't have those, now is the time to start! At least once a quarter, meet with your team to review progress to goals and discuss issues of alignment and/or misalignment. We discussed team conversations in the last chapter. This is a crucial team conversation to include as a regular part of your management discipline.

Aligning the Organizational Structure and Roles

Organizational structure can be a seductive topic in business life. Some leaders may want to give a high performer a promotion, or they want to find a way to move a poor performer (or a troublemaker) out of the organization. Other leaders may be experiencing some other business challenge where they believe a new structure will help. Or, there are those who simply want to re-arrange things for the sake of something new. Moving the boxes on the chart can be such fun, and may give us the illusion that we are making things better for the business!

Don't let my teasing here irritate you. Organization Design projects are among my favorite.

More appropriately, as you set and align on strategies and goals, it may become apparent that you need to make some changes to your organizational structure. Or, as you begin to act on your strategies and goals, you may find that misalignment is occurring too frequently, and suspect your structure is part of the problem. This can be a good reason for reviewing the structure, but there may be other reasons for such misalignment.

There are definitely very good reasons to review and adjust, even completely overhaul your organizational structure as your business changes and grows. Strategy/goal alignment is one of the best, but here are a few others:

- Mergers, Acquisitions or divestitures
- Cost Reductions
- Changes in process
- Growth
- Market or regional changes

Therefore, when I am asked to work with clients on their organizational structure, I most often propose starting with an assessment process, to understand fully what is happening in the business. Here is the process I usually use, with appropriate customization to the unique needs of the business/industry. I certainly did not create this process on my own, but learned it from key authors and mentors in the field.

Assess the Current State. It is important to understand clearly the current state of the business, on several dimensions, when moving into a project like this. It not only gives insight into why a re-structuring is necessary (or not), but also sheds light on the particular type of structure to build, and on what other aspects of the business to address. In Organizational Alchemist language, we call this an *organizational diagnostic.*

Like most of us in the field, I use a couple of very well known models to help organize my diagnostic process, such as the Galbraith "Star Model™" or the McKinsey "7S™" framework. Galbraith's Star is a really simple model assessing the state of the organization against the categories of Strategy, Structure, People, Process and Rewards. The McKinsey 7S model is almost as simple, just with more components, including Strategy, Structure, Skills, Style, Staff, Systems and Super-ordinate Goals.

The way I use these models in diagnostics does vary, however, depending on the client and the presenting issues when we first meet. I often interview several key leaders in the organization, if not all of the top leaders, plus a few next level people as well. In some cases, I create a little survey tool, so I can get input from a larger part of the population and have a more quantitative view of the outcomes. If the business and the leadership are so inclined, I love to do this as a large group event, or as part of one. Think annual sales meeting, where most of the sales leaders and other key sales people are all present – what an opportunity to get their input regarding key aspects of the business!

Once I've collected the data, then I create a summary report to share with the leadership team, along with a few recommendations to get the project underway. With a diagnostic summary and recommendations in hand, as well as the organization's strategy, it becomes time to sit down with the team and design the organization. By "team," I mean either the full leadership team, some subset of the team, or a combination of leadership team members and a few additional people critical to the organization's strategy and future. Remember my points from Chapter 3 regarding having the right people in the room.

Identify Required Capabilities. The first real step in designing a structure is to ask the question, "In order to achieve our strategy, and to address the issues identified in the diagnostic, what capabilities will we need?" Will merger/acquisition integration be required? Will some new or updated skillset be critical? Will expertise in some process or system become necessary? Will you need more management/leadership capability? What capabilities will you *no longer* need?

Identify those 5-10 most critical capabilities. This doesn't necessarily mean they become the basis of the new structure, but they must be addressed in one way or another to achieve the strategy.

Build the Conceptual Structure. In this step, the team reviews a variety of ways to approach the structure. There are many potential types of structure. A few common types include:

- Functional Structure – where the critical functions are centralized and the business leans on these for productivity.
- Business Unit Structure – where each unique business

operates independent of the others, perhaps integrated by a few standards and policies. This would likely be the best concept for our car wash example, until we might overlay a regional and/or functional hybrid as the company grows.

- Regional Structure – where well-defined geographic regions independently contribute to the overall company revenues, operations, and profit.
- Process Structure – a type of matrix where major business processes are organized into teams across the various functions in the business. For example, the Product Development process would organize program managers and core teams across all the functions in the organization in order to create and launch new products.

The important thing is to draw lots of pictures and charts, without thinking too much about individual people or even trying to build a traditional organizational chart just yet. Think about how the organization should work. It is very likely most conceptual structures will evolve into some hybrid of the above list. Sometimes, two or three potential structures will evolve.

A note on participation here. Of course there are times when I work only with the business leader himself or herself. Sometimes the organization is not large enough to engage the full team in decisions that affect their own jobs. In a few large organizations, there is such strategic change that it is not possible to involve others. Most of the time, however, I recommend involving many in the organization in design decisions.

Select the 'Best-fit' Structure. Having done the conceptual thinking and discussion, map the alternative structures created against the required capabilities identified in the first step. Select the structure that fits the business at this moment in time.

There is no perfect organizational structure. If you happen to create one, it will be imperfect very shortly. Life and business changes too frequently, and no structure adequately addresses every aspect of the business. The key is to select a structure that best fits your needs now, but is also flexible enough to allow for some adjustments over the next year or two. It is as foolish to expect that any structure will be good for the entire life of the enterprise as it is to change the entire structure too frequently just to deal with unique issues or opportunities.

A part of this process is also the work of identifying any key interfaces between organizational units and creating positions or governance that will ensure those interfaces are managed well. For instance, how will unique business units avoid overwhelming or annoying customers with contacts by sales people from each individual unit?

Staff the Top Level(s). Now that the structure is, for the most part, defined, it is time to identify the best leader for each specific component. In truth, managers have a very hard time separating the structural development from the individuals they want to lead the organization. Especially when many of those people are actually participating in the development of the structure! Therefore, the process is iterative. The key is not to design an organization completely around the current leadership. This limits considering the future possibilities for the business.

Given this truth, it will be important to determine how the actual staffing process will happen. Will all the positions be 'posted' for anyone to apply? Will the positions simply be appointed to individuals by the top leader? Will an external search be necessary? How will this staffing process be communicated to the rest of the employees?

One mistake that many organizations make is to carefully organize and staff the top level, or possibly two levels, and leave the rest to chance. This is a major reason that so many re-organizations don't work. People become confused and misaligned with others regarding goals and roles, compromising relationships and productivity. Therefore, a good implementation and change plan, including the re-alignment of all levels throughout the organization, is critical.

Plan for the Change. We'll talk much more about change management in Chapter 7, but there are two things that are crucial to ensuring a successful re-organization – stakeholders and thorough implementation planning.

Stakeholders are any of those people who must be considered in the process of re-structuring. These include internal and external stakeholders. Among these include key candidates for positions, individuals who will be displaced by the new structure, customers who will be impacted by the new setup, employees whose management may change, the board of directors, and shareholders (if you are publicly traded) who may view the new structure as either favorable or unfavorable to their investment. There may be specific individuals who require some special attention, as the new structure is being developed and ratified. A clear and well-thought plan for how to communicate with and address the concerns of stakeholders is a top priority not to be neglected, regardless of the size of the business.

See www.noblealignments.com for a couple of simple tools for identifying and communicating with stakeholders.

Implementation Planning is simply project planning. It is important to ensure the plan includes the stakeholder plan discussed above, plus the plan for ensuring the structure is aligned throughout all levels and across all horizontal functions, regions, etc. This may involve more meetings, either large or small, and further restructuring of departments, teams, etc. It may also involve some training or re-training. Sales groups get impacted here frequently. As companies combine "the bag" or begin to arrange their products into 'kits' for more integrated customer solutions, sales people need re-training in both the products and the sales process.

Much of implementation gets into getting re-aligned on goals and roles, so people don't trip over each other in the newly structured world. So you see, alignment is a constant concern in organizations. People in an organization can do far more than one individual, but they have to stay aligned.

All this is great fun for me, and many managers and HR people as well. But perhaps *the most basic level of alignment,* and the problems that occur when there is misalignment, is in teams. Let's go there.

Effective Teams

I love working with groups and teams. As I shared in Chapter 1, I studied marriage and family counseling, and my clinical training was with groups. While I found therapy and counseling among the most energy draining and hardest work I have ever done, I have found working with groups and teams in business organizations to be among the most energy-producing and fun things I do.

I know. As a manager, sometimes the team can be a challenge. Teams are made of people, each one with his/her own set of characteristics, strengths, experiences and quirks. They get into conflict with you and with each other. They create drama in the workplace and sometimes make productivity impossible.

But on the other hand, it is awesome when they work together! When they seem to produce great results smoothly, and enjoy it!!

There has been plenty of work done in this area, and lots and lots of research. It turns out that those great teams are not just anomalies. There is a framework that allows them to be this way. And, as it turns out, the interpersonal issues are in the tiny minority of reasons that teams are great.

The most commonly used model for building and maintaining effective teams is "GRPI." It's not a particularly catchy term, but it works. It was first developed by a founding Organizational Alchemist named Richard Beckhard. Here it is:

Goals – We've already talked at length about this. Imagine that! Yep, aligning on goals is the very pinnacle of ensuring great team relationships.

Roles – Hmmmm. There's a trend here. Getting roles right is central to team effectiveness, as we noted. We have the right start. Go back to the section on Aligning Organization Structure and Roles for more detail here.

Processes/Procedures – We haven't looked at this extensively here, but it is the absolute next step when designing the effective team or organization. What are the 5-7 core processes that need to work right for the team to function well? Is everyone clear about how they operate? How are decisions made? How are handoffs managed? These questions and more are part of building and aligning everyone on the team processes/ procedures. How is communication managed?

While I have been called to help teams, most often, regarding Interpersonal Relationships, in fact the problems have been much more about Roles and Processes/Procedures.

Interpersonal Relationships – Would it be a surprise to learn that real interpersonal relationship issues account for only about 5% of team effectiveness problems? Most people are surprised, but it is true. When you stop to think about it, it makes sense.

So what do you do with this? You may have guessed – you do a little assessment to find out where the greatest source of team ineffectiveness lies. I use either (or both) interviews or a little survey, then get the team together to review the results and build a plan for change. Sounds simple, but has shown great outcomes. Yes, I've done a little 'therapy' with groups on occasion, but mostly it is this simple process that works the best.

Imagine the return on spending a few hours just to course-correct and re-align the team on what they are trying to accomplish, their processes for doing it, and how they define the roles they have in it all.

A Note on Team Development. It is true that teams don't stay 'built.' That is why "team-building" is such big business. Here is what happens. A member of the team leaves, a new one arrives. Or, a member of the team gets promoted to manage the team. Or, the product/service they perform changes somehow. Or any number of other possible changes occurs, creating a new team dynamic and new reasons for re-alignment. I'm not really covering the stages of team development here, but in some ways the team does go back to an earlier stage of development when something changes. When that happens, it becomes helpful to do a little re-aligning. Maybe you don't go through the full GRPI assessment and improvement process, but perhaps a little mini-session where the team just does a little check-in on the four areas of effectiveness would be helpful.

Well, we've now covered the two MOST fundamental things important to mobilizing people: Mastering Conversations and Aligning Goals, Roles and Teams. These two basically help to stabilize people in a good performing environment. Now, let's get to the things that really energize them, increase the velocity of their contribution, and mobilize them for the powerful organization you envision!

Chapter 5
Grow Talent and Leadership

Our focus here is primarily about growing leaders – meaning those who will take positions or roles that move your organization forward. Most of the time, this means positions/roles where the individual either formally or informally manages people. Formally, these will be true management positions. Informally, they may be project or program managers who must lead across functions. Or, they may be people serving specific positions where they have no direct reports but must lead the organization, such as a single Human Resources or Finance leader. If you have mastered the performance and development conversations from Chapter 1, and you become adept at the capabilities we'll discuss in Chapter 6, then you are doing the right things in terms of growing the general employee population, those on the front lines of production or service.

Unless you are a solo-preneur with no intent to build your business further, you'll need to grow leaders. Whether a small business entrepreneur on a growth trajectory, CEO of a major corporation, or in any role in between, developing leaders who can run the business without you should be among your highest of priorities.

Grow vs. Buy

The question of whether to develop the people you already have, or hire experienced talent from the outside, is a difficult and important decision in every business. There are risks and benefits to either decision. Growing talent from within is typically less expensive than the costs of hiring experienced leaders. Additionally, growing internal talent avoids making mistakes of cultural fit. Externally hired leaders come with perhaps more experience than internally developed leaders, but they may come with bigger problems and differing cultural expectations. On the other hand, it does take time and attention to develop internal people, as well as some financial expense for coaching, assessment, and training. Sometimes internally promoted people have an adjustment period, learning to gain the followership of former peers.

Much of the grow/buy decision has to do with both strategic and operational needs, the available talent pool, and the nature of the business itself. Consider the following questions:

- What is your strategy for growth? Local expansion or dispersed? One product/service or diversified?
- How have you structured your business?
- How fast (or slow) is your business growing?
- Given the strategy and structure, what capabilities and skills will leaders in your business need over the next 2-3 years?
- What are the operational and administrative needs of your business? Will you need more functional leadership or more business development/sales leadership?
- What is your current internal talent pool like? Professional/managerial or operational/hourly? Ambitious and career oriented or "just happy to have work?"

- What is the external talent landscape like, given your industry? Lots of experienced talent looking for opportunities? New industry with few who know how it works?
- What is your timeline? Do you need someone who can perform immediately with little direction, or do you have a few months (or longer) to help someone take full leadership where it is needed?
- How strong is your company culture? Is it the culture you'll need for the future? What will leaders need to understand, and be able to impact, regarding your current and/or desired culture?
- Is the position being staffed a brand new position or business offering, involving activities not covered previously in the organization? Or is it a well-established role with a number of existing employees who may know exactly how to operate?

All these are tough questions that require good thought and discussion, and the answers will be as varied as there are businesses out there. In general, I encourage erring on the side of growing internal talent, but the discussion must be had. If the business is in high growth mode, a 'both/and' answer is probably appropriate. It will require both developing AND hiring to keep up the growth pace. Even then, however, where to place brand new leaders versus where to develop and promote will require discussion of the questions above and more.

Having a discipline of talent planning will help address these questions before the need for a leader becomes urgent and raises the risk of a wrong and expensive decision.

Plan, Search and Develop for Critical Positions

I am talking about traditional succession planning here, and I am not! Succession planning often focuses only on a replacement plan for existing leaders, should they be hit by that proverbial "bus of opportunity" and move on. I am actually talking much more about having a very comprehensive and strategic plan for talent and leadership, a plan for preparing for and dealing with near term, long term AND contingency needs of the business.

This kind of plan does not have to be heavily engineered, although in large organizations it can feel that way. You will have done some of the work already if you have done the organization design/structuring process outlined in the last chapter. Here are the basic steps:

1. Review the strategy, required capabilities and current structure.
2. Identify the 3-20 most critical roles (fewer is better) required to accomplish the strategy now and in the 5 years ahead – longer if you dare.
3. For each of these roles, outline the 5-10 "must have" competencies – both skillset and leadership behaviors – to accomplish the requirements of the role.
4. Internally, assess the talent you have who might most closely meet the competencies.
5. Externally, search the industry (or similar) for individuals who might meet the competencies.
6. Create a matrix that places the identified talent in to 1, 3 and 5-year readiness categories.
7. For each internal candidate, particularly those in the 1 and 3 year categories, outline a development plan based on the outcomes of your assessments.

8. For external candidates, create a "recruiting" plan that builds the relationship with each one.

The steps are simple enough. It is the discipline and effort involved in accomplishing each step that is intense. Unfortunately, it is this intensity of effort that causes senior leaders to neglect the practice entirely. Of course, it also keeps internal HR partners, and me, in business when senior leaders do recognize the need for the practice and see that they need help to execute it!

It is important to think here in terms of roles more than positions. What if the most critical role you will require going forward is not reflected in any position currently in your organization, or is really a front-line position of some sort? I did say that most of the time your plans will address leadership roles, but there are definitely those times when the critical roles are needed deeper in the structure. Also, thinking in terms of roles gets you out of the trap of profiling the person in today's position as the going forward profile. The person filling a position today may not be suited for a critical role in 3-5 years.

Calibrate on Talent Assessment

This is a little about performance management as well as talent planning. The activity here involves a leadership team getting together for the purpose of aligning on their perceptions of the performance and potential of their next level of leaders. In the case of small companies, this could mean a calibrated assessment of all employees. It is typically the central activity in a larger, more strategic meeting regarding talent. These meetings have many names, most including the words "Talent" and "Review" in them. A few of these names in my experience include:

Organization & Management Development Review (OMDR)
Talent & Leadership Review (TLR)
Organization & Leadership Development Review (OLDR)
Talent Review

Some of you may recall that GE called theirs simply "T2," to denote the review in the second third of the year that focused on talent.

Whatever you call it, calibrating on the capability of leadership to take the organization toward its future strategy becomes more critical as the organization changes and grows. By the time a company reaches about 20 employees, and the intent is to grow further, I recommend that some form of talent review process become a part of the annual cadence of business governance.

Most companies choose to use some form of categorization of their employees, relative to their performance, behavior and potential for further career growth. Larger companies even classify these leaders further, making note of their diversity and/or geographic location and mobility.

While there are many tools for calibration being used today, the tool still used most frequently to help leaders assess and categorize employees is a three-by-three matrix, often called a "9-box" or "9-block." One axis of the matrix is used to rate the performance of the employee from low to high. The other axis rates the employee's career potential, typically for achieving at least two levels above where he/she is now positioned, from low to high. Clearly, this is a very simple tool that can, if used well, have great power in directing how talent is developed, moved, promoted, and managed in the organization.

By identifying those with highest potential for career growth, management is able to best invest effort and expense in

	Low-Performer High-Potential	Moderate-Performer High-Potential	High-Performer High-Potential
POTENTIAL	Low-Performer Moderate-Potential	Moderate-Performer Moderate-Potential	High-Performer Moderate-Potential
	Low-Performer Low-Potential	Moderate-Performer Low-Potential	High-Performer Low-Potential

PERFORMANCE

developing leaders for the future. It now becomes clear who to include in succession plans, future site, business or functional leadership. Coupled with the critical position management outlined in the previous pages, it becomes very clear where there is existing talent for the future, and where a broader talent sourcing and recruiting plan will be required.

Now, how do you go about preparing for and conducting a leadership assessment calibration meeting? I'll talk a little about the full Talent Review in a later section, but here is generally what 9-block work should look like:

1. Determine the population of employees you'll be assessing, given the size and complexity of your business.

    In the car wash example, calibrating on the managers and supervisors, then on the rest of the employees might seem most fair. In a 20 person law office, calibrating all the attorneys would make most sense. Comparing the performance and potential of people performing very different roles or functions might not prove so helpful, but it really does depend on the business. Even in the car wash, there could be one car attendant who shows tremendous future potential, and should be discussed for development.

2. For each person to be discussed, have the direct manager/supervisor do some preparation before the meeting.

This is where the results of that performance conversation from Chapter 3 will have come in very handy. The manager can pull examples and specific evidence from the documentation of that conversation to bring to the calibration meeting. The better prepared the direct manager, the better the calibration discussion.

On the other hand, if there is someone a manager has specific criticism about, preparation for that should be done as well. Calibration is about getting the perspective of all the participating managers regarding a particular individual. If there is feedback to be given, it is really important that this be brought up. Sometimes, managers see the calibration meeting as a 'sales pitch' for their favorite employees, and ignore important behavioral and/or skill needs the employee must address for continued success. Everyone must come to the calibration session with a view to how best to serve the company and the employee for the future. Criticism is something to prepare as well.

3. Set an agenda and conduct the meeting.

Be organized about this discussion. Create some basic ground rules regarding how to talk about each employee. Provide time boundaries so no employee is either over-discussed or neglected altogether. Start with highest potential/highest performance first, then middle group, finally lowest performance/potential.

Be prepared for the meeting to take some time. Management is very tempted to neglect talent discussions, but once they get to these meetings, they want to talk a lot about it. I have rarely seen talent discussions take less than half a day. You can divide the meeting into parts if necessary – first meeting just to calibrate the 9-box as a whole, then one meeting for focus on top 5-10, one meeting for lowest 5-10, final meeting for 5-10 middle performers. These could be 2-hour meetings. Once again, how you structure the discussion(s) depends on the size, complexity, culture and operation of the organization.

The meeting should conclude with some instructions to the team regarding what and how to communicate the outcomes for all employees discussed.

4. Focus on how to develop those with the highest potential.

There should be no promises made to anyone who has been identified as high potential to lead the company going forward, but it is important to work with them on a development plan that is motivating and builds the right capabilities for the company's strategic needs. Sometimes, when told of their potential, employees get the impression they now have some promise of a particular position and become frustrated if that does not happen in the time or fashion they expected.

A note of caution here: DO NOT USE a calibrated rating as a form of reward, or just to try to keep a valuable employee who does not really have potential for higher positions! This is, at root, dishonest manipulation of people that *will* be exposed. It will likely result in a disappointed and increasingly disengaged employee you will lose. This is where the need for those honest career conversations discussed in Chapter 3 is critical.

For more about 9-box talent assessment, see www.noblealignments.com

Move Talent Strategically

Having identified your strategy, structure, critical positions and leadership, it becomes more clear how you should move your talent into positions that continue to move your business forward. By use of the word 'move,' I do not necessarily mean *physical or geographic* movement. I don't dismiss it either. What I mean here is where you will position people *next*, in order to ensure you have the right talent in the right places to accomplish the right things for your strategic goals. In many ways, this gets right back to that earlier discussion of Critical Positions.

So, certainly as part of your regular Talent Review (whatever you decide to call it), but likely more frequently, begin discussing 'talent movement' or, to use another term, 'assignment management.' In fact, this should be a major part of development planning with your best people. Today's business environment changes very rapidly, and today's young people often expect to change what they do more rapidly as well. Working in 1-2 year increments is likely preferred to the old-school preferences for a single-direction, hierarchy-oriented career. So, as you plan for the next year or two in the business, think about how to move your people into other positions in ways that will both satisfy their own needs, as well as your strategic direction. Forgive the analogy to a game of maneuvering inanimate objects, but talent movement might be thought of as a sort of corporate chess game – strategic, thoughtful.

In one company, we used the term "Talent Drill" to brand a quick leadership meeting, conducted once every couple of months, to look at positions, strategy and talent, and identify where we could move talent to continue developing their leadership, and the capability of the company. Sometimes these involved international assignments, in other cases, cross-functional or cross-business moves, even specially designed positions were created to accomplish strategic goals and/or projects.

An important consideration here is to ensure you are working with people who are experienced and performing well, yet early enough in their career and life that movement up or down the hierarchy, or across functions and/or geographies is still possible for them without sacrificing their income. Believe me, I'm not being age-discriminatory here, just practical. I have seen situations where the right person had to opt out of a great move because he/she could not afford the financial change. This scenario just emphasizes a couple of things regarding developmental movement of talent into new assignments:

- Sometimes, the best way to develop someone is to give her/him a 'stretch' or even 'hardship' assignment, one that they actually are not quite ready for, but the experience makes them better for it.
- Review and manage talent deep enough into the organization to uncover those people for whom new roles just might reveal greater potential. Don't make the common mistake of managing only the top two layers of talent in the organization.
- Moving people into multiple roles provides them with the breadth of business understanding to help the work more smoothly across complex structures, and to identify where they have the most passion and perform their best, so they don't find themselves in highly paid positions they can't leave but don't love.

Experience remains the best teacher. No amount of education, training or coaching will substitute for what we learn in new experiences and roles.

I think you may now see that by "Move Talent Strategically" I also have a broader definition of 'strategically' as well. Your Talent Strategy is integral and critical to your Business Strategy. To accomplish your business goals and their career goals, your talent must be in the right places doing the right things. Setting up your talent for business success is as important, if not more, as setting up your marketing, finance, sales, or operations strategies.

Integrate New Leaders with Rigor

I love this topic, and I love this practice! I don't understand why so many business leaders neglect to take the time and effort to be sure that new leaders are well-assimilated into their new roles. It is not good business. Why?

- It takes long enough for a new manager/leader to get up to speed, so why let a bad integration make it longer? It can take 6-9 months, even longer in some cases, for new leaders to become satisfactorily productive in a new role. Misalignment on goals, poor starts to peer and/or employee relationships, and other misstarts can extend the adjustment further or even cause a failure.
- The costs of management turnover are phenomenal. Not only are there the recruiting costs, but the costs of training, lost productivity, and employee confusion (even drama?) as well.
- In larger organizations, these costs can be even higher, due to 'normal' attrition. Consider that roughly 1 in 8 leaders will need replaced in any given year. That's quite an impact on your organization.

- In small organizations, a bad integration is obvious to everyone. Who wants to work in a place like that?

Integrating new leaders can be one of the easiest things to do in an organization, yet it still is one of the most neglected. So, how do you do it? I have been part of creating some very elaborate processes and calendars, and there are some excellent books and other resources on the market (see the appendix) but here are the fundamental components of what should be a comprehensive plan for each leader's first 3-6 months in the role.

Stakeholder Relationships – Probably the greatest de-railer of leaders in new roles is their failure to build the right relationships with the complex constellation of stakeholders in their new "universe." These relationships fall roughly into these categories -- boss(es), employees, peers, customers and/or suppliers. Let's look briefly at each:

o   Boss(es) – Of course, we see the necessity of building a positive relationship with the new boss, or in today's matrix organizations, multiple bosses are involved. New leaders need to spend time with each of their "superiors," understanding the priorities and expectations of each one. Taking the time to get very clear here may reveal some conflicting expectations to be resolved in the earliest days, or at least provide fair warning of some of the challenges to be faced going forward. This is also the time in which the leader gets to know the working style of her management, the relationships between them, and how she should plan on working with them to get things done.

o   Employees – When a new leader is announced, whether from inside or outside the team, those who will report to him are naturally a bit anxious. The leader, too, will be anxious to get a clear assessment of the strengths and weaknesses of the team. Therefore, a couple of activities with this group will be important. First, it is common (though not common enough), within the first 5-15 days of the new leader's arrival, to conduct an "assimilation" process with the direct reports of the new leader. Additionally, a person-by-person review and assessment of each employee is conducted.

In the assimilation process, employees are asked a series of questions about the new leader, the team, its goals and challenges, either via a single meeting with all the employees, a questionnaire or interview of each employee, or some combination of these. A summary report is provided to the new leader, and then she responds to the team directly in a single meeting. This is intended to open dialogue between the leader and the team, and to address some important goals and concerns as the leader takes charge.

In the assessment of employees, the leader learns the backgrounds, strengths, challenges and potential of each person, via review of resumés, past performance evaluations, feedback from others, and direct one-on-one conversations with employees themselves. This of course builds the relationships with team members, and helps the leader understand how to best leverage their capabilities and develop them for the future.

o Peers – Our toughest critics, and best friends, are our peers. They can make us or break us in life and in business. Therefore, these relationships may actually be the most important as we move into greater levels of leadership. As leaders, great peer relationships makes it much easier for employees to work across departments, streamlining handoffs and ensuring there are fewer (or none) gaps or major overlaps that can create issues of quality, execution timing, or cost overruns that result when departments do not communicate well.

Meeting with peers, developing those relationships early on, may also help to reveal and resolve confusion about roles and responsibilities, AND it creates more allies and fewer competitors in the world of organizational politics. This is a critical, must-do step in the integration of everyone in a new role, and most of all for new leadership roles.

o Customers/Suppliers – Depending on the role, early discussions with key customers/clients and/or suppliers contribute significantly to confidence and trust in these relationships. These provide the message that the leader is ready to pick up the ball where a previous person left. Where possible, arrange for a transitional meeting that includes the new leader, the former one, and the customer or supplier. Ensuring continuity is the primary goal here.

Goal Clarity and Alignment – The second great de-railer for leaders is goal and role confusion. In the first 100-300 days of a new role, leaders need to spend significant time with their own bosses, getting crystal clear about the goals expected of him/her. Without this, employees will be confused, as will peers, and thus productivity will be a problem. Goals often change between the interviews, day 1 and day 300. Staying on top of this ensures everyone is successful, not to mention the business.

Some leaders feel timid about asking for time with their own managers to get clarity. They believe they achieve certain levels because they are expected to be self-managing. This is true to some degree, but it is also true that every new situation brings many differences where the wrong assumptions can be very disruptive and career destructive. Every integration plan should have a built-in schedule of regular discussions regarding goal clarity and progress. The frequency of these discussions should start high, such as once every two weeks, then decrease over the course of the first year.

Coaching and a Peer 'Mentor' – In the first weeks and months of a role, many companies assign a peer to every new leader, to help him/her maneuver the many dynamics of entering a new environment, role, and relationships. This practice is particularly helpful in larger organizations with strong cultures. It can be tough to "break in" to these environments when coming from the outside. In new and growing companies, as well, this can be a great way to accelerate integration and ensure building the culture.

Stress Management and Personal Balance – In every new situation, there is some level of stress, whether good stress or bad stress. Of course, the newer the situation, the higher the stress, but every new situation brings stress. While it feels very difficult to take the time for self-care in the first days of a new role, the integration plan should include aspects of stress management and personal balance. Where a week-long vacation may seem impossible, planning a 3-4 day weekend every 60-100 days is recommended. Additionally, ensuring regular exercise is also critical, even if only a 30-minute walk, 4 days a week. Or, try walking meetings. Oxygen to the brain can work miracles in mental and emotional functioning!

First 100 Day Assessment – To ensure new leaders stay on track, an assessment at the 100-day mark, or somewhere near it, is a great practice. This typically involves interviewing a few peers, employees and superiors, to understand what is working and what is not. This simple little process can be conducted by the leader him- or herself, or by a trusted objective party, such as a Human Resources partner from inside the company, or an external consultant. The summary report is then shared with the leader and a continuation/correction plan is created and validated with the leader's manager.

Coach, Mentor, SPONSOR

You may have noticed by now that, while this chapter is focused on growing talent, there isn't anything about training. I'm certainly not against it. I love facilitating classroom training courses, and offer them in my own practice – when it is appropriate as part of a larger development and business effectiveness initiative. Why? Because training, while great in its proper use, accounts for only 10% of actual learning for adults. We are grown-ups. We got schooled in many basics as children and young adults. As adults now, learning is about applying those basics in new situations. Therefore, 70% of new learning happens for us by direct experience. The final 20% happens via coaching, mentoring and sponsorship. What do those words mean, and is there a difference? I expect there may disagreement from some of my peers, but here is how I view this piece of the GROW component of M.A.G.I.C.:

Coach – I see a coach as someone able to help build a new or deficient skill or competency, or set of them. The coaching relationship is often, therefore, a very specific and "contracted" one. Consider these as a few example types of coaching:

o   Speaking Coach
o   Writing Coach
o   Start-up Coach
o   Organizing and/or Time-Management Coach

The idea here is that there is something very specific, measurable, and time-bound to be learned. Therefore, the coaching relationship is often short-term.

As a consultant (yet another confusing word we can discuss in a later chapter), I see myself as a coach sometimes, helping leaders and groups to identify and solve specific problems,

Nancy Noble, PhD

teaching them specific skills and capabilities. Sometimes, I go a bit beyond that and do a bit of work for them. Rarely, however, would I see myself as a mentor or sponsor.

Mentor – I see a mentor as more about a relationship than about a skill or competency. There is less measurability in a mentoring relationship, as the purpose is typically to help someone gain capability in less concrete areas, such as culture, organizational savvy, strategic thinking, and so on. There are many models for establishing formal mentoring relationships in organizations, yet there seems to be a less formal "chemistry" and interpersonal depth that makes the most successful mentor-mentee relationships.

In Chapter 1, I mentioned my own mentor. I had been educated and coached through many of the skills basic to this practice I call Organizational Alchemy. My mentor patiently, and impatiently, directed me through many of the twists and turns the practice can take. She showed me my blind spots, whether I wanted to see them or not, and the impacts of not checking them. She consoled and encouraged me through failures, but always asked how I would avoid that happening again. In my own experience as mentee, the mentoring relationship is rarely comfortable, but completely trusting, open, ego-shattering and confidence-building.

For the mentor, therefore, there must be more in it for them than simply teaching a skill or capability. The aggravation and personal investment in such a relationship must have some return in seeing the mentee grow and learn, watching them stumble, fall, then run. To engage in relationships like this, some level of connectedness (dare I say emotional intimacy?) seems important for their ultimate success. This seems especially important when we look at the life-cycle of many mentoring relationships, where the mentee develops and must move on to successes without the mentor's influence. This cycle may include some conflict and separation issues. That depth of trust and connectedness is necessary for the relationship to survive the changes.

Mentoring, therefore, while at the core of leadership development, is a bit tricky and requires some care when creating formal programs. Building these programs in organizations requires good structure to begin with, including some education of mentors and mentees, ground rules and boundaries-setting. And, while the success rates, in terms of the numbers, may not ever look great, the levels of success achieved by those few truly successful relationships may far outweigh the investments made in the program.

Sponsor – I see a sponsor as a kind of 'personal promoter,' someone with influence willing to help open career doors for the person sponsored. A sponsor may be a mentor and/or coach, or may be simply a fan of the individual's capability and potential. All leaders should see a part of their role as one of sponsoring growing leaders. Talent management processes should absolutely include sponsorship practices at least as part of succession planning and management. Good sponsors:

o Have a position of power and influence important to the future of the person sponsored.
o Show interest in, and build some relationship with, the person sponsored.
o Have a network of people to whom to introduce the person sponsored.
o Make introductions and recommendations to projects, positions, and other opportunities for the sponsored individual's career growth.

In rare cases, one individual may be coach, mentor, and sponsor for a leader. For most of us, however, a number of people fulfill these roles in various ways.

For every potential leader in your organization, the important thing to do is to understand what the development needs are, then identify whether the need requires coaching, mentorship, or sponsorship, and then help identify the right person to fulfill that role.

This clearly takes a bit more thought and effort than sending them to a training class, but the returns are so much greater for both the individual and the company.

Regarding Personality and Leadership Assessments and Exercises

So, what about all the assessments we put leaders through? How do they fit into the M.A.G.I.C. formula? Like training, I am a fan – a big fan – when it is appropriate.

Leadership assessments come in many forms, as we'll review below. Each assessment, even within a particular category, should be selected based on the specific purpose for which you wish to assess leaders. Often, a 'suite' or 'battery' of assessments is assembled to accomplish specific developmental purposes. This should also be done with caution, so not to overwhelm leaders with so much information about themselves that they do not know where to begin.

Leadership assessment is actually a science in itself. I recommend engaging a consultant with this kind of background to help design your program and assessments. Here are a few of the types of assessment to consider in the process:

Personality 'Style' Assessments. There are a multitude of these. Some are well researched and highly marketed. Others less so, but worth the investigation. Style assessments are typically most useful to help leaders understand their own preferred ways of operating, communicating, and leading. They are also used with teams, to help team members understand each other a bit better, and to communicate and relate more effectively with each other. Sales teams also like to use style assessments to help them understand their prospects and clients as well.

In my opinion, style assessments should NOT be used for hiring purposes. While some styles may be more suited to certain types of work, it is dangerous to make hiring and/or promotional selections based on style. The better criteria for these purposes can be assessed in other ways, as we will discuss later in this chapter.

Style assessments are typically of great interest to people. Who doesn't want to know more about their favorite subject – themselves! Let's be pragmatic about it as much as possible, though, since we are talking about business. Here's a brief review of several instruments, some highly popular, others less well-known but still worth a look.

o   Myers-Briggs Type Indicator® - Most often referred to as the MBTI®, this assessment is the most popular and most widely researched tool in use today. Interestingly, it began back in the 1940's because Katherine Myers became intrigued that her new son-in-law seemed to see the world differently than she was accustomed. It measures one's preferences along four fundamental ranges of thinking and behavior:

Introversion vs. Extraversion (I/E)
iNtuition vs. Sensing (N/S)
Thinking vs. Feeling (T/F)
Judging vs. Perceiving (J/P)

The assessment reveals one as expressing one of sixteen combinations of these 8 preferences. There is a long form and a more abbreviated form of the assessment, and there are multiple excellent activities and tools available for teaching and facilitating training and team events. The tool is used heavily in leadership and executive development. Every Organizational Alchemist should be familiar with MBTI® and be able to use it.

It is the first style assessment I was introduced to while in graduate psychology studies, and I appreciate its value and the research behind it. I do still use it on occasion, typically when the client specifically requests it over others I might recommend. I have personally found that there are other tools more simple and practical to use in business life.

o   DiSC® -- Perhaps the second most popular among style assessments in business, DiSC theory was created by William Moulton Marston, with his 1928 book Emotions of Normal People. (He also invented the first functional lie detector polygraph and created the Wonder Woman comic – smart guy, eh?) Later, the DiSC® Profile was developed for use in clinical and business applications. The four themes of DiSC® are

(D) Dominance,

(i) Influence,

(S) Steadiness, and

(C) Conscientiousness.

There are some complicating factors involved when studying DiSC® more deeply, but many sales organizations love to use it as the four types seem simpler than perhaps is MBTI®. There is also much research behind it now, since it has been around a few decades, and more continues to be done. Therefore, there is high confidence in its validity and reliability.

o   Insights Discovery® -- This assessment is newer, developed in the 1980's. Many know it as the "colors" assessment, as it uses the themes of Cool Blue, Earth Green, Fiery Red, Sunshine Yellow to categorize its four types. Like MBTI® and DiSC®, it is based in Jungian typology, which might also be connected all the way back to Hippocrates and his four body-fluid based temperaments.

The validity and reliability research for this instrument is also strong. It carries an advantage of high simplicity, while still providing deep insight into oneself and, perhaps, others. Many companies are moving to this assessment for team effectiveness.

o   Opposite Strengths® -- This is a personal favorite of mine, so be warned that I may not be objective enough about it. My own dissertation research is related to this assessment and how people prefer to learn. I've worked with many couples and teams using this assessment. The theory was developed by Jay Thomas, a management consultant, in the 1950's. The premise of the theory is more related to success than to categorization of type. The concept is that success is not about what type someone is, but about how flexible one is to use ALL their strengths in the right timing. I personally consider it to be a development model more than a personality model.

The personality "patterns of strength," as we call them, are based in three pair of opposing positive strengths: Thinking vs.

Risking; Practical Thinking vs. Theoretical Thinking; and Independent Risking vs. Dependent Risking. One's combination of three "lead strengths" results in one of eight core patterns. Much of what the system teaches focuses on how to 'flex' to other patterns when situations and relationships call for us to use different strengths than our lead.

I must say, though, as much as I love the concept and the tools, there is a level of complexity that makes many business people impatient. They want something much simpler and more memorable, particularly in their relationships with others.

o   B.A.N.K.® -- So, in response to what I've heard from business experiences, I have come to see this newest tool as highly simple, memorable, and practical for many business settings. Developed by a sales professional, Cheri Tree, in the early 2000's, this assessment is intended to help identify the buying values of prospective customers and clients. Cheri was intrigued by what she learned from the other typologies, but was frustrated that it didn't seem to help increase her sales. She then noted what various prospects seemed to see as important, then categorized those values into four primary "codes" – (B)Blueprint, (A)Action, (N)Nurturing, (K)Knowledge. She asked prospects to prioritize four simple cards. She then customized her own behavior and conversation to match her prospect, and her sales increased exponentially.

B.A.N.K.® training programs teach participants how to 'code' others with whom they are engaging, then teaches how to customize their behavior and conversations to ensure optimum rapport and influence. This is highly practical in sales training, but has some positive effects in other relationships as well. There is also new research on the instrument, validating it as predictive of buyer behavior. This research also found that,

understanding what is least or even not important to the other person is as critical as knowing what is most important. It makes sense that good relationships are sensitive to both what is offensive to the other person, as well as what is attractive.
I've recently been using BANK® most frequently, and have had some very good client successes with it, primarily for sales, customer relationships and people management. It is absolutely worth investigating for sales, and may prove further use in other talent and leadership applications going forward.

These were but a few of the many personality style tools available. My intent has been to introduce them as a great means for helping people with self-awareness, other-awareness, and communication. Now, on to other tools for development…

360-degree Feedback – When used properly, 360-degree feedback can be the most helpful tool for developing leaders, from my perspective. Like standing in a 3-way mirror, it is hard not to see all one's strengths and weaknesses when getting the viewpoints of our peers, superiors, employees, and sometimes customers.

There are fundamentally two ways to go about this. Both ways begin with getting very clear about what key competency/skill areas on which to get the feedback.

o   Interview – While very labor-intensive, this method is the most informative. One or more interviewers are engaged to conduct interviews, taking very precise notes on very specific open-ended questions. Here's the basic process:

Meet with the person being assessed and his/her manager. In this meeting
•   Identify the 5-7 core competencies/skills to be assessed

- Identify at least 3 people each among peers, employees, customers, superiors, to be interviewed in addition to the manager.

- Establish the schedule for interviews, report and development planning

Create the interview protocol based on the identified competencies/skills
Conduct the interviews 1-on-1, either face-to-face or via teleconference, taking copious notes on the responses. Guarantee the interviewees confidentiality. (more about this later)
Build a detailed summary report and share with the individual first, then the manager.
Meet to determine a plan for leveraging strengths and addressing opportunities for learning and improvement.

o   Survey – There are many existing 360-degree survey tools, most of which can be customized to the specific needs of the individual and the company. Additionally, there are consultants who can help to build survey tools completely unique to the culture and success criteria of the company. Purpose is everything. Get clear about the major reason for the assessment, then choose the instrument and process based on that purpose.

The steps for a survey are exactly like the process for interviews. The two main differences include:

- Competency selection – In the case of surveys, the key competencies for focus should be the same for all feedback recipients. This helps in terms of ensuring consistent cultural expectations, and in terms of providing additional aggregated data to the broader organization. Having this information regarding the primary strengths and development needs of all your leaders and/or potential leaders makes development planning and budgeting much simpler, and allows for some group learning opportunities. It also informs leadership regarding how any cultural changes are progressing or stalling, based on the competencies expressed by the leadership population.

- Reporting & Interpretation – Since survey questions are in multiple-choice format, building the reports is a much simpler task. There is not the need to summarize lengthy interview responses. Survey reports provide the quicker 'snapshot' of a person's strengths and development areas, whereas the interview data provides much deeper insight.

Culture and Climate Assessments – These assessments could also be discussed in the next chapter, but the point here is that leaders create cultures and climates, intentionally or not. These assessments help people understand the kind of culture/climate in their own teams, to allow them to understand whether this is the desired environment or not. Culture or climate is really about the unwritten rules by which the team or organizations is operating. Key categories for climate assessments include:

- o Communication practices – what to say and what not to say, and when
- o Career Management and Growth – what actually happens
- o Workflow and process management
- o Relationship within and across the teams

Again, these can be conducted via interview and/or survey, although a survey will be most practical in the majority of companies.

Assessment Centers/Simulations – When evaluating key talent for high level promotional potential and opportunity, the use of assessments centers is common. This is a rigorous practice for the evaluators and an intense experience for the individual being assessed. It is expensive for the company sponsoring the assessment. Therefore, it is reserved for those most high potential individuals. And, as I've said before – purpose is everything.

The process includes interviews, surveys, psychological assessments, and simulated work exercises. Typically, the simulation and psychological assessments take 1-2 days of very intense activity, facilitated by highly trained and experienced assessors. The report offers a robust view of the individual's capabilities, and highlights the key areas for development.

These are often used in the process of selecting people for senior level promotions. The important thing, though, is not the selection aspect, but the development issues to address whether or not the person is selected for a specific opportunity.

- A Note on Confidentiality – Many assessments require the feedback of others in order to get the most helpful results. This can be a sensitive request. Some will not feel comfortable giving completely candid feedback if they believe their responses will get to the individual and create problems in the relationship. Therefore, assuring confidentiality is critical. I want to make a distinction here. "Confidentiality" is not "anonymity." In the case of 360-degree feedback, in particular, the names of respondents are often known. We cannot guarantee anonymity in most cases. However, we can assure respondents that we will hold their specific responses confidentially, not attributing specific comments or item responses to specific individuals without their permission.

Historical Interviews – The final form of developmental assessment I'll describe here is the 'historical interview.' Executive recruiters have made this tool popular as a means of making selection decisions. Additionally, though, it is a great way to identify key strengths and development areas in order to build a solid development plan. The process is pretty simple, albeit intensive.

o   Arrange for a lengthy interview with the individual being 'assessed.' Typically these can take 3-4 hours, so it may be helpful to split it into two meetings.
o   Begin with early work experiences – yes, like in high school and/or college – and go forward from there. Ask questions like:

What was the job? What were your main responsibilities? What did you like best about that job? What did you like least?
If I were to ask your manager from back then, what would he/she have to say about you as an employee? What would you say about that manager?
What did you learn most in that experience?

o   After completion of the interview, ask what kinds of things the individual saw as key themes. Draw your own conclusions.
o   Identify a few key strengths that have continued through the individual's history, and a few development areas. Discuss what to do next with the information.

While this seems tedious, most find that there is tremendous insight to be had from this kind of exercise.

Wow! We covered a lot of ground in this chapter. But, after all, the G is the central letter in our M.A.G.I.C. formula. Leaders who do not grow their talent cannot grow their business.

Now, how do we keep all this talent really engaged in their work – 'on fire' if you will – so they go well beyond just carrying out their duties, but really making a difference for the company? How do we keep them enthusiastically committed to stay with you now that you have invested so much in developing them?

Chapter 6
Ignite Active Engagement

For much of the last ten years of my experience internal to corporations, I led company-wide 'Employee Engagement' efforts. This usually started with an intensive survey, measuring employees' levels of commitment to their work and the organization by asking about things like their intent to stay with the company, the quality of their relationship with their manager, their belief in positive career growth with the company, and so on. We typically provided the results to each manager, assuming she/he had more than 5 responses. The corporate level data helped us predict turnover levels and understand what key 'driver categories' we should improve as a company in order to keep employees positively committed. For the managers and their teams, the results helped understand what key areas were causing employees to be engaged with, or disengaged from, their work, the team, and the organization.

While this was all great information, and I highly recommend the discipline of annual or bi-annual surveys, there was always the challenge of how to follow through on the information they provided, how really to engage managers in the practice of engaging their employees!

You can research "employee engagement" online and find multiple studies connecting company financial and operational performance with high levels of employee engagement. It is a well-proven fact that employees who are 'emotionally committed' to their work and their organization tend to perform better, thus producing better company outcomes. But, that is about the employees and their engagement – not about a survey!

Our discussion here, therefore, is primarily about how leaders can build and maintain a team and/or company environment that "sets afire" the hearts AND minds of their people. We can talk about surveys in the next book.

What's Engagement?

I looked up the word 'engagement' in several sources. Those definitions were all pretty boring, frankly. They mentioned things like "appointment" or "obligation." To me, they sounded much like the definition of "employment," not really the kind of attitude and spirit we tend to think of when we really want someone to show high energy, enthusiasm, inspiration and determined action in their work.

To solve for this, most in the corporate world would define 'employee engagement' as "emotional commitment" and an engaged employee is often described as using "discretionary effort," getting closer to what we look for. Let's consider the whole concept for a minute. This concept is much less concrete than what we have discussed before now, but very important.

Think about those times when you have been completely 'consumed' with some project or task. By consumed, I mean you were so deeply involved in the task that time stood still, you were actually having fun, and you were totally committed to achieving the satisfaction that comes with successful completion. Your purpose for doing the task was completely aligned with what is most important to you. THAT is the kind of engagement we are talking about!

So, let's consider that an employee who shows such engagement as on F.I.R.E.™!

F – Focus. Engaged employees are highly focused on their work and on helping their organization achieved the highest possible results. This focus leads not only to better productivity and performance, but also often generates innovative ideas.

I – Initiative. Engaged employees feel such a sense of commitment that they often will take action without being directed, perhaps even without asking permission! They empower themselves to see situations and take the actions necessary for success for the business, team and the organization. They accept accountability and ownership before it is asked of them.

R -- Results Orientation. These employees don't just take action for the sake of action. Initiative and performance are all directed to a final result for which everyone is working. They remain fully aware of, and committed to, the goals and strategies of the business, directing the focus of their own performance toward those outcomes.

E – Energy. All this focus, initiative and results orientation is conducted with a level of energy obvious to everyone. They may not be skipping down the halls, but their pace, tone, and overall appearance is magnetic, even contagious! Engaged people often inspire others, thus igniting and spreading the F.I.R.E.!

THAT is the kind of environment that brings massive business results and makes people love working in your organization!

What Lights F.I.R.E.?

How does that kind of engagement get sparked?

Now think about the environment that allowed you to be so focused, so energetic, inspired and committed. What were some of the characteristics of that environment? Were you free to think and work in your own 'style?' Did you experience a sense of support and encouragement from your manager and/or others around you? Were there others available with whom you could brainstorm, even collaborate to create the best solutions? Was there recognition for your efforts, in the right proportion to the achievement?

I expect you are dreaming of alphabet soup by now, with all my acronyms. Well, the bowl just got bigger, and there are more to come! Let's think of the engaging environment as F.U.E.L.™ for the F.I.R.E.™

I recently had the privilege of working with a small company during a staff retreat in Telluride, Colorado. We stayed in this beautiful mountain home with an enormous fireplace. It snowed about a foot while we were there, so the moment was right to take advantage of that feature. We bought a few boxes of pre-cut firewood and some starter sticks. When we opened the wood, we were pleased to discover that the wood had been cut into kindling, tender and log-sized cuts. This enabled us to start and keep a roaring fire in that fireplace throughout the afternoon and evening. Not a bad way to debrief some of the work they had been doing both together and independently!

My point? Because we had all the different cuts of wood, it was easier to keep the fire going large and long than it might have been had we had only one size cut. The same is true when we talk about engagement. It is the combination of drivers that make the difference. There are lots of well-proven lists of engagement drivers, founded by solid research with all types and sizes of organizations. Just like there are lots of sizes of wood to fuel a physical fire, there are some fundamentals.

Starting engagement F.I.R.E. is one thing, keeping it going requires:

F -- Fulfulling Work. I'm not talking about attractive and high paying jobs here. Not every job is a job to be loved. A trash collector may not love the task. A manufacturing operator may be bored by the repetitive nature of the duties. A customer-service agent may be frustrated by customers who behave badly. Yet any of these people could say their work is fulfilling, due to the contribution they see themselves making to the business. The most engaged employees see that what they do matters to the overall purpose of the organization, and the organization recognizes that contribution as well. They also see that their contribution not only pays their own bills and helps the company's bottom line, but also makes a difference to the people served by the company – be it trash-free homes and businesses, useful products of every kind, or fixing the situation where the company may not have met customer expectations.

Whatever the job, at whatever level in the company, leaders fuel engagement by helping everyone to see what they are actually contributing to. In my work in the bio-tech industry, I saw every kind of job, from CEO to factory workers measuring plastic tubing. The highest engagement scores were most often in those areas where leaders had been clear about the contribution the team was making to patient care, safety, and healing.

It's basic, like fire tenders. People work to put food on their tables and clothes on their backs. But their work is better quality, higher energy, more productive, more fun when they see that their work matters.

U -- Upgrowth Prospects. I know. I had to do some thesaurus work to get a 'U' word for career development and learning. It really is a word! I kind of like it, though, because it doesn't seem to assume that learning is always hierarchical. When we "grow up," it is not about position, it is about learning and accomplishing what is most important in our own lives. Engagement is not limited to those who see themselves, or are seen by the organization, as "upwardly mobile." Engagement is fueled when people see that they are learning and growing, whatever the structural position they have. Some of us want to get really deep in our field, learning every theory, methodology, toolset and practice. Others want to move up the ladder of responsibility and position, while others may simply want to lead and influence those around them without a title.

Engagement is fueled when people see there are a variety of opportunities of learning and upgrowth in their organization. Today, we see lots of movement of young people from one company to the next. Their search is for continued learning, growth, and fulfillment, as we have already discussed. Those companies who have employees on F.I.R.E. have environments and opportunities for people to learn and grow on and off the job.

During my days in the high tech industry, the senior HR executive in the division I was part of would say, "The way to develop someone is to put them in a job just before they are ready." In my mind, that is upgrowth. Give people projects, tasks, or positions that stretch them, that give them new knowledge, capabilities, and/or skillsets. Look for ways to continue to grow employees. When they see that the organization is committed to their development, they stay to see what they can learn next, and they become ignited.

E -- Encouraging Management & Co-workers. That fire we built in Telluride required just a little more than the right kinds of wood. We would periodically go over and poke on the logs, moving them around a little to give more air to fire so it would stay aflame. People are like that too. We need friends and interested managers to provide an ear for ideas or rants, a hand for occasional help, a word of support or a little verbal prodding. We are not machines. We are people with emotions and egos, both of which need either stoked or brought down to reality. If we do not have these people around us at work, the engagement fire is not quite so roaring. If we do have them, we think twice before going somewhere else, because they serve as the "oxygen" we need to perform, produce, contribute and grow.

L -- License for Autonomy. To keep the flame of engagement burning, it must be okay for a person to have some level of autonomy and self-direction. This may vary, based on the industry and job, but it is essential kindling to ensure continued engagement. I mean a little more here than simply the absence of 'micro-managing,' though this certainly is part of my message. Engaged people stay engaged when they have learned that taking initiative of their own, and having the license to accomplish a goal with their full input and personal ownership, is not just okay but completely encouraged and favorably recognized.

Even in those roles where there is high regulation and quality control, there are ways to build in autonomy. This, in my view, a major part of the success of programs like Six Sigma, Lean

Manufacturing, quality circles, and other similar participative methods for ensuring quality and productivity. These kinds of initiatives help to fan the flames and keep people engaged in their work. Injecting License into the environment contributes significantly to employees feeling they have Fulfilling Work. Having even a small amount of autonomy in one's work allows the feeling of "this is MY work," something to take ownership of and in which to take pride.

What Dims Engagement F.I.R.E.?

So, how do people get disengaged? You've seen it, or felt it yourself. Over a period of time, an employee loses that bounce in his/her step, the energy level begins to drop, productivity and behavior changes begin showing up in a way that you don't want. Sometimes the changes are gradual, other cases are more acute and an employee may become "actively disengaged," contributing to an environment that reduces everyone's enthusiasm and drive, perhaps even becoming hostile.

Disengaged employees are bad business. They become the "dead weight" in organizations, and sometimes become poisonous. They call in sick more, work less productively, sometimes create drama and recruit others to join in their discontent.

When we made that fire in Telluride, we knew we didn't want it going all night, so as we began to wind down our evening, we just stopped adding wood and moved the remaining wood around so the various pieces would not continue to feed the flame. Isolating the wood pieces allowed the heat to dissipate, burning down the wood and damping the fire. Had we felt we needed to put the fire out faster, we might have just doused it with water. That's what happens with disengagement. There are multiple causes and multiple speeds.

Most of the research out there shows that, even with all the right F.U.E.L., people can become disengaged. There can exist some factors in the environment that actually smother the F.I.R.E. Yep --that means more alphabet soup! Here's how to S.M.O.T.H.E.R.™ employee engagement:

S – Surroundings. Working conditions that do not allow for safe, healthy productivity will discourage engagement. Tools and equipment that are outdated, don't work consistently, or are otherwise insufficient to accomplish the tasks will frustrate employees and drain their energy enough to disengage them. Even inefficient, overly bureaucratic, cumbersome processes can be a problem for keeping people focused and engaged.

M – Money. When people are worried about pay, benefits, time off, and other areas of their personal situation, it can become disengaging. Of course, the organization can't control some aspects of this, but the lack of, or insufficient, health benefits, retirement planning options, and other compensation may not only disengage employees, but may make you unable to compete for the talent you need.

O – Others. Bad relationships at work are a real threat to engagement. Most of the time, poor interpersonal relationships are a result of other problems we've discussed in this book, like goal and/or role misalignment, process challenges and other work-related issues. Fixing these can actually improve interpersonal relationship. Relationships with direct supervisors and management are also very important. People don't always leave a company because of their manager(s). But a less than satisfactory relationship between manager and employee can definitely dampen engagement F.I.R.E. and cause a person to begin thinking about finding somewhere else to contribute.

T – Treatment. This one can be pretty serious. When people feel they are being treated unfairly, even abused, they can't focus on much of anything else. Bullying doesn't just happen among children. It happens at work, by peers, managers, or others. There are, of course, the extreme cases of sexual harassment, or other discrimination based on age, sex, ethnicity, religion, sexual orientation, and so on. But there are more common abuses that must not be tolerated in order to avoid a disengaging environment. These abuses include public criticism, yelling or cursing at another employee, unwelcome teasing, or other verbal and/or physical behaviors that create an environment of intimidation, fear and hostility. And don't discount the impact an environment of 'FUD' can have on engagement. That is, Fear, Uncertainty, and Dread. Frequent layoffs, unexplained firings, or performance management processes that create destructive competition between employees just to try to keep their jobs will stamp out engagement quickly.

H — High Control and Competition. Control and competition are often qualities of a healthy business, until they are not! When the controls are so high that people do not feel autonomy in any aspect of their work, engagement will decrease. The same is true of competition. When there is very high competition, and the incentives for teamwork and cooperation are low, then engagement is decreased. People are creative and social beings. They don't respond well to being viewed as machines, nor do they tolerate environments where everyone is pitted against each other.

E – Exiguous Communication. New word for me, too! Exiguous. It means "limited, scanty, meager." Get it now? When people don't know enough about what is going on, they check out. If the company doesn't engage with them, why should they engage with the company? In fact, what often happens is, well you've heard the adage – "In the absence of information, people make stuff up." And what they make up usually isn't good. I hope you are clear that communication is much more than the perfunctory email when some change comes about. Good communication is multi-directional, involving people in dialogue to ensure clarity. It is also strategic, giving focus to the right things about which to communicate and how much or how little communication is needed. Great communication won't ignite engagement, but it sure keeps disengagement from spreading.

R – Reputation. That is, the reputation of the organization. Who gets excited about working for an organization with a bad reputation? No one wants to brag about that, nor do they want to spend lots of energy contributing to company success, unless they have enough F.U.E.L. to cause them to want to be part of changing that reputation. Think of the big banks back in 2008, or Enron. When those scandals went down, employees became disengaged, some actively so, and many left. On the flip side, consider modern "cool" companies like Google, Apple, Zappos and others. Their reputation alone helps them keep a pipeline of talent waiting to get in, and those who are already in are, at a minimum, pleased to say who they work for. A great reputation won't guarantee you engaged employees, but a bad one will probably disengage them.

Here is my final point. Just like a fire cannot be started with wet wood, it is very difficult to create an environment high engagement until the disengaging elements are cleared up. Take a good look at your organization. Be sure your efforts to F.U.E.L. engagement F.I.R.E. are not wasted because you have not addressed those things that could immediately S.M.O.T.H.E.R. it.

Engagement and Powerful Organizations

I won't spend a lot of time here, as many others have the robust research that proves my comments. I'm proposing here that engagement is an essential force for powerful organizations. What we see in the research is this: Not all companies with highly engaged employees are among the most successful businesses, but most successful businesses do have highly engaged employees. To be a powerful organization, employee engagement is a requirement, not an option.

In the M.A.G.I.C. formula, the 5 forces do have some interdependency. Engagement, therefore, may be ignited as a result of the other four forces, or it may become part of the cause for one or more of the others. The reverse could also be true. Disengagement may occur due to neglect of the others, or may cause the dissolution of one or more of the other four forces. Do not discount or neglect the power of engagement. Commit to being a F.I.R.E.- starter organization.

Oh, and if you do want to look further into conducting an engagement survey with your company, go to www.noblealignments.com, contact me and let's talk.

We've got just one more force of M.A.G.I.C. to look into AND only one more acronym!

Chapter 7
Change Readily – well T.I.M.E.D.!

Long ago, I was told a story about a couple who went to see a marriage counselor. When the counselor asked, "How do you deal with change?" one of the partners replied, "Oh, we have this big jar and we just throw it all in that jar every night." Like you, hopefully, I thought this was a pretty funny misunderstanding of the question, but the double meaning of the word may not be so far from the experience and practice of many of us when it comes to the changes we experience in life and work. Sometimes, changes happen to us, and sometimes we make those changes intentionally. When they happen to us, it is not uncommon to try to just ignore them, throwing them in a metaphorical 'jar' until the jar is so full that we either deal with all the change or deal with the consequences of refusing to deal with it, or both.

Have you ever made a transaction somewhere, paying in a large bill, and the vendor could only make change for you in some massive collection of coins? There you stood, with both hands full of metal, forced to figure out what you were going to do with all of it. That, frankly, is a little too much like our world today. There are changes coming our way faster than ever, forcing us to respond and figure out which ones to leverage for our best use, which to embrace right away, and which to "put in a jar" until we have the energy and wits to assess, organize and leverage them.

So, in the M.A.G.I.C. formula, we focus on the force of change in organizations, the timing for change, readiness for change, leading change, change resilience and the process and mechanics of purposeful change.

Well T.I.M.E.D. Change

Perhaps the most important thing about managing change is knowing when it is time to make a change in the first place. In our coin storage example, if we raid the jar too frequently, our savings do not add up very quickly. If we wait until the jar is running over, we have to do some cleanup and organizing in order to bank what has been saved. With all the changes occurring in organizations, it is a skill to understand and respond when the time is "just right." To help this decision, here are four most important situations in which change should be well managed. And, yes, it is another acronym! Change is well-T.I.M.E.D. in the cases of ....

T – Technology. Process automation, new business systems, and digitized marketing approaches are definitely moments where focused, intentional change management is critical. These technological changes, and more, create needs for new organizational structures, role definitions, training, process clarity, goal alignment, and strong communication within and outside the organization.

In my work inside a large company, I remember the challenges faced between several functions when we entered the realm of digital marketing. This impacted the design of marketing campaigns, collateral, budgets, sales practices, product management and more. The change was subtle at first, then like being handed $45 in coins, we found ourselves having to work through interdepartmental conflicts, role confusion, wasted marketing funds and other challenges. It was definitely a time to step back and build a clear plan for change.

Technology changes our lives and business very frequently. When new technology enters the picture, whether electronic or very manual, it is time to plan and lead a change effort.

I – Inconsistent or Inadequate Success. It is a bit of a paradox, but sometimes, gaining stability, or sustainability, requires change. When the business is not succeeding as desired, then something must change. This often means changes to strategy, processes, structure, people, business models, even higher-level goals and vision. You may say, then, when is it NOT time to change? Should we ever be satisfied with the success of the business? Well, yes and no.

There is always room for improvement in every business. Most successful companies are always ready to make incremental changes to keep them up-to-date and competitive. It is true that these improvements may require some level of change management. But when leadership looks at their metrics, as compared to their goals, and there is a big gap, it is time to make more significant changes that either stabilize results or catalyze major jumps in business outcomes. In these times, it is important to be very intentional and disciplined about how change is promoted and executed. These are the times when business units, functions, or whole enterprises call on someone like me to help. In the cases of incremental change, there is less need to be so intentional or to call on additional resources.

M – Mergers, Acquisitions, Divestitures, Restructuring. Next to big technology shifts, as we have already discussed, this is the time in when companies most often experience the need for intentional, disciplined change management. Structural changes can be highly distracting and counter-productive, due to the many people, cultural and operational implications. This is a major part of the reason for high rates of undesirable turnover in the first year after these kinds of structural activity.

Many leaders make the mistake of restructuring their organization only at the top, leaving the rest to the leaders below them. This leads to confusion and misalignment, creating doubts about the efficacy of the new structure. I consider an organizational structure as "finished" when at least two levels below the top have been structured and aligned across functions and/or businesses.

Mergers, Acquisitions and Divestitures, at least those of some size, seem to present the heaviest change management activity. In mergers and acquisitions, there is high complexity in making the decisions regarding "who wins" in terms of systems, operating processes, talent, and so forth. In divestitures, the issues are similar, although the separating organization typically has much more of the change to manage, because they often experience "starting over" concerns, determining their own choices of systems, operations, customer management, and so on.

In my own experience, I was a participant in a major divestiture, few minor acquisitions and a major one that was effectively a merger. I also participated in a major divestiture. As you might expect, how the people in the organization(s) felt about the whole process was somewhat dependent on what side of the deal they were on. Those in the acquiring or divesting company showed higher levels of engagement and enthusiasm about the future prospects of the newly forming company. Those who were being acquired were less enthusiastic, and often became disengaged. Those in the company left after divestiture may have realized some budget challenges or other loss, but typically did not seem to feel much impact at all. We'll talk about this again later in this chapter, but the thing to note is that change plans will need to be customized to the unique needs of all parties in these complex situations.

E – Entry/Exit. When a company enters or exits a market, product or service offering, it is time to change, and to be intentional about managing that change. In these situations, not only does the structure of the organization change, but there is a change in the types of talent required. Adjustments in the sales force and their training are necessary. Customers must be consulted and assisted through the transition. And more.

Consider the magnitude of the change when IBM began to focus more on services and software and then left the hardware business! Think of that change – International Business MACHINES left the machines business altogether! Yes, there was a period of time involved here, but the changes were highly complex and required new ways of operation, and a new culture, throughout the company.

D – Disruption. The very word itself says things have changed, and therefore the organization must respond. Market disruption is frequent today, though we know of a few very significant disruptive events. Wireless technology, the internet, cloud computing. These technology disruptions have both created and destroyed whole industries. Walmart's disruption in distribution strategy helped consumers afford more of the things they need and want, yet in many small towns it contributed to the demise of the local retailer. Oh, and remember those big movie rental stores? All are gone with the advent of streaming video via Netflix, cable or satellite, and mobile technology. Book, music and office supply stores are starting to look very different today than they did even two years ago. Apple's iTunes and Amazon's Kindle have totally replaced the bookshelf and the boom box.

Disruption can't always be noticed or predicted, but it is always a time to change, and do it quickly. Seeing disruption is a new skill of survival in our markets today. It is the reason I added the 'D' to this acronym, rather than leaving it at simply T.I.M.E. Disruption is perhaps the most important basis of well-TIMED change. In my opinion, IBM saw that it had missed its opportunity to be successful in wireless and mobile technology, so it just skipped that step in order to stay competitive, opting to play in services and software. Barnes and Noble tried to catch up after Kindle began to rise, offering its Nook. However, the Kindle application has dominated e-book sales. Both these companies had been successful in their respective industries, yet disruption caught them and required response. IBM's change may have been smarter, and has helped them stay more competitive, than was Barnes and Noble's, but disruption caught them both.

Knowing it is time to change is critical. Well-timed change wins!

Change Leadership

Business leaders often relish their roles as the ones to see changes and disruption, and to alert the organization and mobilize them. Where they often fail, however, is in providing the resources and time to actually execute to the change. By the time the organization is just accepting and working the change plans, the leaders have moved on to something new. This can create frustration and disengagement, so it is important that leaders monitor and assess their own role throughout the process of a major change.

Leaders do not necessarily need to be the project managers of change. Their role is to ensure the organization is able to stay focused both on current operation and on ongoing changes. Therefore, while someone else may be the 'arms and legs' of change, the leader must be the 'voice and ears' of change.

Huh? What I mean here is, business leaders have just a few, but extremely important, things to do in a change process:

• Inspire – Leaders must be the primary voice of inspiration to make a change. It is their job to help the organization to see why there must be a change in the first place, and what the world will be like after the change is complete. This is not a one-time effort, however. Leaders need to be consistently visible, even repeating themselves frequently, to keep people focused on the real outcomes that are the purpose of the change.
• Listen – Throughout the change, leaders must be able to ask good questions, and to listen to their teams as they report on progress, challenges, wins and losses throughout the change.
• Support – Leaders need to be ready to make a decision when the change requires them to do so. They also need to be ready to support the decisions of those involved in the day-to-day tactics of change, staying aware that they may be guilty of slowing change if they second-guess the actions of those actually working to execute to it.
• Celebrate – When a key milestone is reached, leaders should be the first to celebrate wildly, to help the organization see how much closer they are to the desired future, and to loudly reward their efforts.

As leaders do these things, the mechanics of change can be given to others, along with the power to make the change effective.

Framework for Change Management

There are some excellent frameworks and toolkits out there for planning and executing to change. I don't really propose a new one here. Rather, I want you to understand the main components of these frameworks so you can begin to plan your change, or so you know the basics to look for when you begin to seek the help of an expert in change management.

Change Platform
The first and FOUNDATIONAL step in change is to get very clear about why there is a change necessary, what the change is, what the company will gain from the change, and how much change is really required.

Most clients ask for my help because they need or want some sort of change. "Why?" is my first question. What problem are you seeking to solve with a change, or what goal are you trying to reach? Why is it important to make this change now, as opposed to a year ago or a year in the future? The rest of the platform follows pretty naturally from there.

I say this step is foundational, because there is really no reason to begin a change project without it. There should be undeniable clarity in this platform. It will serve to keep everyone focused and engaged throughout the effort. Change is expensive and takes much energy and effort. The platform for change should provide the motivation to keep going. People will need to have full view of the payoffs for their efforts.

Change Levers & Stakeholders
Once the platform is clear, then it becomes much more clear what to do, how to get it all done, and who will be most important to the success of the change. In this step, therefore,

you will identify all those levers that will ensure the change is executed well. Here are some of the typical levers you'll need to "pull" for change success:

Communication (not just one-way emails and town halls)
Training
Organizational Structure and Governance Practices
Rewards
Performance Metrics & Plans
Processes to improve or create
Systems to implement

Stakeholder management is a major aspect of change management. We've got a section dedicated to this coming up. Good stakeholder management doesn't necessarily guarantee change success, but bad stakeholder management guarantees change failure.

Executing Change
Not much more to say here. Change management is very much about project management. Execution is the key. The problem is often that project managers don't know enough about change management and do not give sufficient attention to leadership issues or to stakeholder management.

Assess & Adjust
Periodically through the change, it is necessary to stop for a minute (probably more like a couple of hours) to review how execution is going and how that is actually effecting the change you were looking for. In the plan should be periodic reviews to assess progress, respond to challenges, and adjust plans as needed. This includes not only the plans around key levers and stakeholders, but also around leadership.

Stakeholder Management – The Critical Ingredient for Change

Next to leadership, this is the greatest "make or break" challenge in making organizational change, and often the most neglected. In every change there are individuals and/or groups who stand to "win" and other who stand to "lose." Or at least they perceive the change in that way. This is true from the very smallest organizations to the very largest. And, there are those individuals and/or groups who can help or hurt the progress of the change. It is important to understand all these people and groups, in order to leverage their help, minimize any blocks to progress, and address the concerns of winners and losers alike.

Once a change platform is clear, and in parallel with designing your change levers and plans, identify the individuals and groups (yes, by name!) impacted by the change and conduct a little analysis of each one, and what actions you'll need to take. Yes, this is a lot of work! Think about what could happen, though, if you don't do this. Does this smell a little political? It should. If you are part of a group, even of two, there are politics to consider. That's not a bad thing, unless it is managed badly.

To conduct this analysis, there are some pretty detailed planning tools out there, which I would actually recommend in those very big changes. Most of the time, though, it helps to begin with a simple two-by-two matrix where on one axis you assess the amount of influence the individual or group has on the change, and on the other you assess how supportive of the change you believe that individual or group to be. This is a fun and productive thing to do in a group, to gain the various perspectives of key members of the change leadership and the project team.

Once you have completed this little (or big) chart, prioritize and address the concerns of these individuals and groups as follows:
- High Influence/High Support – Leverage
- High Influence/Low Support – Communicate & Convert
- Low Influence/High Support – Appreciate & Retain
- Low Influence/Low Support – Large Scale, One-Way Communication

Of course, your plans will need to be a bit more specific than this, but hopefully you see the appropriate attention to be given, and to whom

I said in an earlier section that good stakeholder management doesn't necessarily guarantee the success of a change. It can certainly help, though. If you don't manage stakeholders well, you may actually convert high supporters to low ones, ensuring that the change will fail.

Change Readiness and Change Resilience

One last topic before we leave the C in our MAGIC formula. In the world of organizational change we see these two terms frequently. Here's how I see them.

Change Readiness. This is a practice and a discipline. This is all about the mechanics of creating and executing to a change platform, as we discussed a couple of pages ago. It is all about project management and getting everyone really ready to make the change with as few hiccups as possible. It is the tactical application and activity of a change framework.

Change Resilience. This is about mental, emotional and social attitude and habit. Resilience is that capacity to respond to, even embrace, continuous change. It is that habit of mind that does not accept the concept of "change fatigue," but rather absorbs change and learns from it. When faced with a new change, even a disruption, the most change resilient person will see this as a new challenge, even opportunity.

Change Readiness is definitely easier to "teach" than is Change Resilience. Readiness is a skill. Resilience is a choice. Helping people to understand that resilience is absolutely a conscious choice can make many changes easier to endure.

With that, I leave our review of M.A.G.I.C™. These 5 forces can make the difference between a stagnant, even declining organization and one that is thriving, growing and powerful.

Now, let's wrap this up by looking at the person who practices this MAGIC, the Organizational Alchemist. What is the mindset and "posture" one must take, whether a leader/manager or a consultant/specialist, in order to effect M.A.G.I.C. in his/her organization/client.

Chapter 8
The Person and Mindset of the Organizational Alchemist

Part of the magic of M.A.G.I.C. is the person practicing it. It isn't quite enough to know these 5 forces and use the tools that execute them. There are mental habits and a personal "posture" to assume in order for the magic to be fully realized. In my world of HR and Organizational Effectiveness, we call these 'competencies.' Across my own apprenticeship and journeyman experiences, these are the most important qualities that have allowed me to see somewhat magical outcomes.

Confidentiality

Confidentiality is the pinnacle expectation of the Organizational Alchemist. Without it, there is no magic to work. For consultants, breaching confidentiality is a reputation and career killer. For leaders, such a breach is a big black eye to credibility and trustworthiness, and a major injury to employees' faith in the organization.

When in doubt, do not divulge confidential information. Be cautious about what is visible to others in email and shared documents. Always remind those with confidential information to keep that promise. Do not succumb to any pressure to reveal a confidence.

In very rare cases, you may need to bring another party into the situation, and may feel the need to share a confidence. If there is no express permission to do so, proceed with extreme caution and be sure there is true "need to know" and the person with whom you are sharing is completely trustworthy. These situations are *extremely rare*, so if there is any doubt in your mind, err on the side of keeping the confidence to yourself.

"Hero by Proxy"

In my first years at Motorola, Gary Langley, the leader of our local Organization Development team, held three primary expectations for us all. The first was confidentiality. The second was the posture he called "hero by proxy." His intent was that we not seek personal recognition or acclaim for the successes of our clients. Our job was to make them the hero.

Working M.A.G.I.C. is not for show. It is a team sport. This not only applies to consulting geeks like me, but to business leaders as well. Yes, we see the books written by the "heroes" of corporate America, but if you read what's in them, you'll see that none of them brags that they did it alone. A powerful organization is a "we" thing. It is more often done in a group, not huddled in a consulting office with the top leader. There are a few times for that, but most frequently, there is group input and conversation involved.

Fearlessness

The third of those first expectations Gary made of us. There are times when you will need to pull up a bit of courage in order to effect the changes your organization/client needs. The courage required will vary. Sometimes, you'll need to speak a painful truth in order for the organization to see the need for change. Other times, you'll need to take on a project outside your typical comfort zone. Still others, you'll need to make on-the-fly changes to plan.

One time, I had to pull together a meeting using a strategic framework I had never used before, all with about thirty-six hours notice. Another, I took on a major survey project where the failure of a previous attempt had cost the project leader's job. In still another, I requested a last minute redirect to a meeting with about 40 people in it, then facilitated a risky conflict-management session. I have often had to speak a truth very clearly to an individual client or client group. This typically gave them the courage to do what they already knew needed to be done. Thankfully, these all did have a slightly magical result! Besides the good use of skills and frameworks we've discussed in the five forces of M.A.G.I.C., I believe it was also good exercise of most of the qualities we are discussing here, particularly Fearlessness, Hero by Proxy, Organizational/Political Savvy and Positive Expectation.

There have definitely been times when fearlessness did not work out so well for me. Typically, these were cases in which I failed to exercise an awareness of the greater impact, or when I did not use good organizational/political savvy, both of which we'll discuss below. So, just like the five forces of M.A.G.I.C., one of these qualities may not work so well in the absence of the others.

Positive Expectation

The greatest quality of the Organizational Alchemist is well-practiced positive intent and positive expectation. I learned, way back in my days at the City of Austin, that when I spend even a miniscule amount of time thinking about how a group will respond and how productive they will be, it makes monumental difference in the success of whatever I'm doing with them. I don't really talk about it. I just spend a bit of time envisioning a positive, productive, powerful experience.

Esoteric as it may sound, I am a total proponent of the axiom "You get what you think about." If you expect the organization to be resistant, they will be. If you expect them to rally around a change, they will. Quantum physics tells us this is actually science. Religion tells us it is faith. Those are good, too. I just personally like to think of it as magical and powerful.

The danger here is that, if you spend time thinking about what you don't want, you'll get that!

Learn to practice envisioning great things for your organizations and clients, and the great M.A.G.I.C. you'll do with and for them.
It will be VERY hard to be a successful Organizational Alchemist without this practice.

Curious Observation

This one is fun, but can be challenging. The posture I'm talking about here is one of a slightly awkward, split consciousness. At the same time it is important to be a committed partner with the organization, a part of the effort; it is also important to be a detached observer of the organization's behavior and operations, apart from them.

Observation is a very practiced skill, I'll grant. But it is also an attitude and posture. The intent here is to stay detached enough to notice subtle things in the organization and stay curious as to why those things exist and how to break the hypnosis it seems to evoke.

Huh? Well, let's consider the regular staff meeting and perhaps an experiment. Whether or not you are the leader of that meeting, participate in the next two or three from a position of curious observation, while also continuing to participate in the meeting as you always have. Make note of who speaks first, how people enter the room, where they sit, how they respond to each other and to you. Observe your own behaviors in these same ways. Make copious notes, then review these notes to see any trends or patterns in behavior. THEN, in the fourth meeting, make some slight change in your own behavior – where you sit, the order of the agenda, how you look at a particularly annoying member of the team, or whatever. Don't announce this change, just do it. Keep taking your notes, noticing what happens throughout the meeting. Do this for a few meetings as well.

This little experiment may only give you practice in observation. But my hunch is that it will also show you the value a little curious observation will provide in understanding patterns and group dynamics.

I learned much about this during my counselor training. We had to listen intently and watch closely as individual clients, couples or families shared their troubles with us. We had to show empathy with the client in their pain, while at the same time observing what was going on underneath the surface. This served me well as I moved forward into my training as an Organization Alchemist.

To be a great consultant, facilitator, coach, or leader, this is a fundamental skillset and posture. It takes significant energy, but in the metaphor of magic, it directs the wand in the right patterns to ensure your spell works. Curious observation directs you to ask the right questions, facilitate discussions toward the right objectives, and recommend the right M.A.G.I.C. interventions.

Synthesis

This is the ability to pull together seemingly unrelated concepts, ideas and/or patterns, to connect them and make meaning of it. It is the ability to catenate, summarize, interpret and act on the multiple parts of a specific problem, challenge or strategy.

The most frequent and fundamental use of this ability is when facilitating meetings. Much of the magic you can bring to a group is helping them to, well, understand what they are talking about! In so many meetings, the participants talk passionately about their viewpoints on a particular issue, trying to win everyone to their own view, yet not seeing the connections between everyone's thoughts.

Similarly, the use of synthesis is required when conducting any assessment or survey process. In the case of leadership assessments, the ability to synthesize interview responses, survey data, and simulation exercise data helps leaders prioritize the key strengths they should leverage, and the critical few development areas to improve on.

Without the ability to synthesize information and behavior from a variety of sources, organizations become bogged down, even confused to the point of paralysis. In today's high information environments, synthesis is key to survival for sure...and perhaps even competitive disruption.

Awareness of Larger Impact

Beyond the concept of global thinking, this is the capacity to look at a decision or action and envision the implications it will have for a wide range of stakeholders and operations. It is the ability to 'predict' how a decision or action may impact individuals and/or the financial, operational or customer aspects of the organization. Rather than a knee-jerk response to a new idea, it is more like your own radar alert system!

For the Organizational Alchemist, it is also the ability to ask questions related to larger implications, and to use good tools and facilitation to note those implications and address them. In change management, in particular, this is an important part of assessing stakeholder implications, and in evaluating and executing to each lever for change.

Like most of the others, this capability improves with experience, but there can be a few "hard knocks" lessons along the way. Admittedly, this has been one of the tougher ones, yet most rewarding, for me. We learn more about the systemic impacts of things the more we learn about the organization, industry and environment. I have found, though, that the little radar begins to activate more and more quickly over time, even in brand new company, sector, industry and cultural environments.

Organizational/Political Savvy

This capability is VERY much like stakeholder management in change, and like the impact awareness above. Yet, it cannot be assumed that is everything. The pre-eminent capability of the Organizational Alchemist is that of navigating *through* the organization to get things done *for* the organization.

I've actually saved this one until the very end (yep, this IS the last one!) because it is that important. As I think I have said a few other times here, the Organizational Alchemist does not do this M.A.G.I.C. in isolation. It will never work. The very inclusion of the word "organization" says many other people must be involved in engaging these 5 forces. Therefore, this capability is that sense of how to communicate and behave in ways that accomplish your objectives with a variety of people and groups in the organization. It is that very fine-tuned skill in interpersonal and political relationships for the purpose of influence to the goals you hope to achieve. Yes, this can be overused and become the negative, 'slimy' kind of politics we all detest.

But the savvy to get things done is among the most appreciated skills in any group. If some change is to happen, if M.A.G.I.C. is going to take place, knowing whom to influence, how to influence them, and when, will make everything go much more smoothly.

Nowhere have I said the people you will influence must be likable. It helps, but it is not necessary to like those whom you are influencing for the greater good of the organization. Nor does political savvy require any dishonest or other unseemly behavior. What it requires is the solid use of all the other capabilities described here, exercised in a very strategic way and in a manner that addresses the core values and needs of those whom you are influencing.

Okay, that's it! At least for now. You now have a base understanding of the M.A.G.I.C. formula and who you must be to use it most successfully in your organization. To help you get started, take the assessment on the following pages.

We'll talk more about tools and skills in the next book. Until then, keep an eye on www.noblealignments.com for continuing additions of tools, articles, blogs, etc.

Now go work some M.A.G.I.C. at work!

Is Your Organization M.A.G.I.C.?

The following assessment should help you understand your strengths and opportunities as you seek to bring more MAGIC to your organization.

M – Master Conversations for Top Performance

Item	NEVER 1	Rarely 2	Sometimes 3	Mostly 4	ALWAYS 5	No Idea 0	Doesn't Really Apply
M1 Performance conversations occur frequently. We don't wait until an annual event.							
M2 We are not afraid of tough conversations with each other							
M3 We have regular 1-on-1 conversations							
M4 Career conversations are true dialogues about employee strengths and weaknesses aligned to company needs.							
M5 Team conversations are highly creative and participative.							
M - Totals							
M - Average							

A – Align Goals, Roles and Teams

Item	NEVER 1	Rarely 2	Sometimes 3	Mostly 4	ALWAYS 5	No Idea 0	Doesn't Really Apply
A1 We invest time and effort to ensure we are all aligned on the strategy and goals of the business.							
A2 We use a disciplined process when structuring and re-structuring the organization.							
A3 Our teams take time to assess their alignment on goals, roles, processes and interpersonal relationships.							
A4 We rigorously evaluate the strategy and environment when considering whether to re-align our structure]							
A5 A good change plan is a standard part of the process when we re-align our structure and/or teams.							
A - Totals							
A - Average							

G – Grow Talent and Leaders

Item	NEVER 1	Rarely 2	Sometimes 3	Mostly 4	ALWAYS 5	No Idea 0	Doesn't Really Apply
G 1 Whether to develop talent from within, or hire them from outside, is a strategic discussion for us, more than a discussion regarding personalities.							
G 2 We are methodical and thoughtful in our discussions of when, where, and why to move talent into developmental positions.							
G 3 We have a rigorous process for integrating new leaders into the company and their roles.							
G 4 Our culture expects that leaders coach, mentor and sponsor talent with good potential.							
G 5 We are thoughtful about why and how we use talent assessment methods and tools, choosing appropriate tools for their intended purpose.							
G - Totals							
G - Average							

I – Ignite Active Engagement

Item	NEVER 1	Rarely 2	Sometimes 3	Mostly 4	ALWAYS 5	No Idea 0	Doesn't Really Apply
I 1 We regularly seek to understand the levels to which our employees are Focused, taking Initiative, Results-Oriented and exhibit high Energy.							
I 2 It is important to us that employees see their work as Fulfilling, including some level of License for Autonomy in every job.							
I 3 There is an environment of Encouragement across the organization.							
I 4 Our people see multiple opportunities for their learning and career growth with our organization.							
I 5 Our leaders work very hard to mitigate those things that might S.M.O.T.H.E.R. engagement in the organization.							
I - Totals							
I - Average							

C – Change Readily – Well T.I.M.E.D.

	Item	NEVER 1	Rarely 2	Sometimes 3	Mostly 4	ALWAYS 5	No Idea 0	Doesn't Really Apply
C 1	When communicating major changes, we help the organization see the clear purpose and strategic rationale for the change.							
C 2	Our leaders exercise their role to inspire, listen, support and celebrate throughout key change efforts.							
C 3	We practice a disciplined method for managing changes in the organization.							
C 4	Our change management efforts address the issues of BOTH Change Readiness and Change Resilience.							
C 5	When making changes, we are rigorous about understanding stakeholder issues and managing them appropriately.							
	C - Totals							
	C- Average							

SCORING SUMMARY

M.A.G.I.C. Force	Average Score
Master Conversations	
Align Goals, Roles, Teams	
Grow Talent and Leadership	
Ignite Active Engagement	
Change Readily – well T.I.M.E.D.	
Overall Average	

Still unsure where to start? Then start with Master Conversations and Align Goals, Roles, Teams. Work these for at least 6 months, then do this assessment again.

Bibliography

The following have influenced my thinking and practice in the field of Organizational Development over the past 25 years, and thus this book.

Most of these are classic works in the field. For other interesting and related books, articles, videos and blogs, go to www.noblealignments.com.

Beckhard, Richard. "Optimising Team Building Efforts", Journal of Contemporary Business, Summer 1972

Benton, Stephen, Schurink, Corine van Erkom, and Desson Stewart. University of Westminster Business Psychology Centre, 2008. www.wmin.ac.uk "An Overview of the Development, Validity and Reliability of the English Version 3.0 of the Insights Discovery Evaluator."

Denison, Daniel. Jossey Bass Wiley, 2012. *Leading Culture Change in Global Organizations: Aligning Culture and Strategy.*

Galbraith, Jay R. and Kates, Amy. Jossey Bass, 2007. *Designing Your Organization: Using the STAR Model to Solve 5 Critical Design Challenges.*

Howell, Ryan T. San Francisco State University Personality and Well Being Lab, 2015. "B.A.N.K.® Development and Validation Study."

Kotter, John P.   Harvard Business Review Press, 2012. *Leading Change.*

Lawler, Edward E., III and Worley, Christopher G., with Creelman, David. John Wiley & Sons, 2011. *Management Reset: Organizing for Sustainable Effectiveness.*

Lombardo, Michael M., PhD and Eichinger, Robert W. Lominger Limited, Inc. *2006   Career Architect Development Planner, 4th edition.*

McGregor, Douglas.   McGraw-Hill Companies, 2006.   *The Human Side of Enterprise: Annotated Edition.* Updated and with new commentary by Joel Cutcher-Gershenfeld.

Marston, William Moulton.   Harcourt, Brace & Co., 1928. *Emotions of Normal People.*

Myers, Isabel Briggs and Myers, Peter B.   Davies Black Publishing, 1997. *Gifts Differing: Understanding Personality Type.*

Nadler, David A. and Tushman, Michael L.   Oxford University Press, 1997. *Competing by Design: The Power of Organizational Architecture.*

Peters, Thomas J. and Waterman, Robert H., Jr. Harper Collins, 2004. *In Search of Excellence: Lessons from America's Best-Run Companies.*

Thomas, J.W. and Thomas, Tommy. Opposite Strengths, Inc., 2011. *The Power of Opposite Strengths: Making Relationships Work.*

Tree, Cheri.   Codebreaker Technologies, LLC., 2015. www.bankcode.com *Video Introduction to the B.A.N.K.® Sales Personality System.*

Ulrich, Dave, Kerr, Steve and Ashkenas, Ron. McGraw-Hill, 2002. *The GE Work-Out: How to Implement GE's Revolutionary Method for Busting Bureaucracy and Attacking Organizational Problems – Fast!*

Weisbord, Marvin R. Jossey Bass, 2012. *Productive Workplaces: Dignity, Meaning, and Community in the 21st Century, 25th Anniversary 3rd Edition.*

www.ingramcontent.com/pod-product-compliance
Lightning Source LLC
Chambersburg PA
CBHW062013200326
41519CB00017B/4785